Abo

Martin McKenna is the author of the bestselling *The Dog Man*. He learned about dog behaviour in a very unusual way: as a boy growing up in Limerick, Ireland, he escaped from family violence by running away from home and living in a barn with a pack of stray dogs. By observing these street dogs at such close quarters, he learned the unique psychology and language shared by dogs all over the world. Now he is passionate about helping dogs and humans communicate more successfully with each other.

WHAT'S YOUR DOG TELLING YOU?

WHAT'S YOUR DOG TELLING YOU?

Martin McKenna

ABC
Books

The ABC 'Wave' device is a trademark of the
Australian Broadcasting Corporation and is used
under licence by HarperCollins*Publishers* Australia.

First published in Australia in 2011
by HarperCollins*Publishers* Australia Pty Limited
ABN 36 009 913 517
harpercollins.com.au

HarperCollins*Publishers*
Level 13, 201 Elizabeth Street Sydney, NSW 2000, Australia
Unit D1, 63 Apollo Drive, Rosedale, Auckland 0632, New Zealand
A 53, Sector 57, Noida, UP, India
77–85 Fulham Palace Road, London W6 8JB, United Kingdom
2 Bloor Street East, 20th floor, Toronto, Ontario M4W 1A8, Canada
10 East 53rd Street, New York NY 10022, USA

National Library of Australia Cataloguing-in-Publication data:

McKenna, Martin.
    What's your dog telling you? / Martin McKenna.
    ISBN: 978 0 7333 2936 4 (pbk.)
    Dogs – Psychology.
    Dogs – Training.
    Dogs – Behavior.
636.70835

Cover design by Design by Committee
Cover images by shutterstock.com
Typeset in Sabon 10.5/15pt by Letter Spaced
Printed and bound in Australia by Griffin Press
70gsm Classic used by HarperCollins*Publishers* is a natural, recyclable product made
from wood grown in sustainable plantation forests. The manufacturing processes
conform to the environmental regulations in the country of origin, New Zealand.

12 11 10   14 15

Contents

Introduction

How I Learned to Communicate with Dogs as a Boy

You could say I was born into a litter of pups.

This is because in our large family of eight kids, I'm an identical triplet along with my brothers Andrew and John. My dad always used to call the three of us 'a litter of pups'.

We grew up in Garryowen, Limerick, in 1960s Ireland — and while Mammy was a beautiful German woman who always worked hard and struggled to raise us eight kids as best she could, Dad drank — a lot — and often became violent.

As you can imagine, it didn't help his temper that I had ADHD (attention deficit hyperactivity disorder), it rains a hell of a lot in Ireland, and we kids were often cooped up inside because of the weather. Dad's hangovers weren't improved by my racing around our house making far too much noise, or stealing money out of his pockets while he slept in his armchair. As a result, I'd often find myself curled up with our two German shepherds, Major and Rex, in our coal shed, recovering from yet another flogging. Dogs came to mean comfort and warmth for me — and these two dogs really did become my best friends.

Needless to say, I didn't do well at school. What with ADHD, a traumatic home life, and some fairly brutal teachers, I couldn't understand what was happening up on that horrible nightmare of a blackboard. The teachers thought I was being a wilful, bold little bastard — but I wasn't. I simply couldn't stop my mind from whirling around and being distracted by everything around me. It didn't help that my brothers seemed to be able to concentrate while I couldn't. It wasn't long before my teachers were beating me with leather straps.

However, this young dog eventually got sick of being hit.

It all came to a head one day when I was in the final year of primary school. The teachers decided my reading and writing skills were so bad that I needed to return to baby class, which was our name for kindergarten. I couldn't believe it: in front of everyone I was taken to the classroom where all the little kindergarten kids were and, amid much laughter, I was seated in one of those tiny baby wooden chairs. Never before had I felt more humiliated.

I decided I'd had enough. Before anyone could stop me, I jumped through the open window and ran back home to my dogs.

Gee, it felt good striking back at those mocking, bullying teachers for once. I knew I was *really* going to get flogged for this — but what the hell, I was having fun. Now it was me laughing at the helplessness of the teachers — and all those cruel, mocking kids.

Things got even better when Mr K and Mr C rolled up in a car and stood at our front gate, threatening me with the leather strap if I didn't get into the car immediately.

'Oh yeah?' says I. 'How are you going to make me? I've

got two German shepherds here. Step inside the gate and I'll let them off.'

They ignored my advice and stepped inside our gate.

It felt great releasing the dogs. Good old Major and Rex chased them out, biting them badly as those two bullies bounced off our gateposts, racing back to their car, threw themselves inside and roared off.

Aha. My first great victory against the world. Thanks dogs!

Then Mammy arrived home, wiping the grin instantly from my face. The dogs raced to the coal shed and hid — but I wasn't quick enough to escape. She was just about as furious as I'd ever seen her.

A couple of weeks later my brothers and I came home from school for lunch to find the pound man had already put Major and Rex in his van and was just about to drive away. We knew that could only mean one thing. The dogs were going to be euthanised for attacking the teachers. Furious and upset, we tried to stop the van from driving away by banging away on it with our hurling sticks — but it kept going.

Distraught, we turned to our mother. I can still hear her words ringing in my ears today.

'Martin,' she said, 'this happened because you set the poor dogs on your teachers. Now you have to pay the price.' That's when it hit me: I was responsible for having my two best friends killed.

My brothers and I were crying because we felt so angry and helpless. Our mother said we had to be strong and go back and face our tormentors — the teachers and other kids at school.

Sure enough, Mr K was waiting for us at school with a smirk.

He cleared his throat as we entered the classroom. 'All right, class — let's have a minute's silence for the triplets' dogs,' he said, and then laughed in my face. Everyone else laughed too.

That was it as far as I was concerned. Humans were cruel creatures and I wanted nothing more to do with the lot of them. Not long after, I ran away from school and home to live an old hayshed that belonged to a farmer called Sean Cross.

The shed was dry and warm if you snuggled down in the piles of hay. Every day — unbeknownst to Sean — his angelic wife, Eileen, would bring me out a bacon sandwich and a steaming mug of tea. My brothers would also bring over whatever food they could scrounge from home.

To avoid running into humans I used to walk the streets of Garryowen at night. On these night walks I would make friends with the town's stray dogs. Soon I had a pack of about five strays following me around and sleeping in the hayshed with me. To begin with there was a shaggy Irish wolfhound-cross, a terrier-labrador cross, a cocker spaniel mongrel, a Belgian shepherd and, lastly, Black Dog — the massive, bad-tempered Newfoundland-cross. I never really gave any of the other dogs names, only Black Dog.

The dogs were great company and they certainly stopped me from feeling lonely on all those long, rainy nights. They accepted me for who I was. They didn't care that I was hyperactive and couldn't read or write. They didn't put me down, torment me, bash me, laugh at me or think I was stupid.

4

To keep them around, I used to get them food. I did this by sneaking into Brendan Mullins' slaughterhouse at night, sneaking past his big guard dog, Buddy, and stealing dog meat from the bins out the back. This was the meat he used to sell to the greyhound men.

As you can imagine, these stray dogs came to depend on me as their sole supplier of food. Soon they never left my side.

It was during this time that I was able to observe this pack of strays up close. We lived together, ate together, walked together and slept together for warmth. With no TV or radio around, there was nothing else to do except watch those dogs interacting and communicating with me and each other. It's not surprising that I soon ended up learning their language. As I'll show you, it's an incredibly easy language to learn — especially if you've grown up speaking English, German and Gaelic, like I did.

So this was my family and we were a pack.

However, I quickly learned that life doesn't always run smoothly in a dog pack — especially when I kept interfering in the natural order of things. Dog fights would break out suddenly when I tried to be fair and share out the food so we could all eat at the same time like a real family. Arguments would start if I tried to make one of the more dominant dogs give up his nice, warm sleeping spot to a more submissive dog that I felt sorry for. Sometimes dogs would attack each other if I started giving too much attention to the wrong dog.

I soon learned there were clear rules in the Dog World that had to be obeyed — or you got bitten. The main rule I learned is that every pack has a dominant leader and every other dog is ranked one by one in a hierarchy below this all-important leader. This meant that, as much as I wanted to create my own little family, I couldn't create a little democracy. *This is because no-one can ever be equal to anyone else in the Dog World.*

Unfortunately, I was so desperate to create my own little family in that shed that I continued to stubbornly treat all the dogs as equals. This meant the shed was constantly erupting into horrible dog fights. The only way I could break them apart was by hitting them with my blackthorn stick until they stopped fighting. Afterwards, I would sit back with my heart going a million miles an hour, wondering why we couldn't all be friends.

Eventually I had to accept that equality is a totally foreign concept to dogs. Once I accepted this and made myself the leader, then ranked the dominant Black Dog below me, and the four other dogs below him, one after the other, then *finally* peace reigned in our shed.

As the leader I had to have everything first and the best of everything. Second best was given to Black Dog — and so on down the line until every dog got its share. It always amazed me that a group of dogs that could be so aggressive when the rules were broken could become so peaceful once the rules were followed. It soon became clear to me that in the Dog World following the rules meant peace and order, while breaking the rules meant instant chaos.

One day I got bored of living on my own with just dogs for company and returned to living with humans. I eventually travelled around the world, ending up married to a wonderful, gorgeous Australian woman with whom I have four beautiful, intelligent kids. We bought a small farm and have a pack of rescue dogs of our own.

Wherever I'd travelled, I'd helped people with their dogs — usually translating what their dogs were trying to tell them — and when I settled in Australia I kept spreading my ideas. One day I was working with a vet and her dog in Bangalow, northern NSW, when Fiona Wylie, a local ABC radio presenter, walked in with her own dog, Rickson.

Well, I showed her I could translate what Rickson was saying and she invited me to be a guest on her radio show. We were an instant hit — the switchboard was always jammed with callers. I was soon doing radio shows all over Australia.

Not long after, I had a book published by the ABC called *The Dog Man*. Not too bad when I still couldn't read and write at the time. Thanks to all my loyal radio listeners and through word of mouth, it became a bestseller.

Now due to popular demand, I've written this second book, *What's Your Dog Telling You?*

I'm proud to be able to say that over the years my wife has taught me to read and write — and this time I was able to write this book almost by myself! Not bad for that little kid in Garryowen who used to stare up at the blackboard in misery, eh?

I believe this book is even better than my first. In fact, I believe if you own a dog then this book is going to change your life.

Now I have the opportunity to take you inside the Dog World and finally get you thinking effortlessly like a dog.

I can translate in my own words what your dog is *really* trying to tell you with its behaviour. I've also provided plenty of tried and tested ways you can solve your dog's behaviour problems.

Better still, I've now got the chance to teach you dog language — one of the easiest languages in the world to learn. This means you'll be able to start communicating directly with your dog in a way it can truly understand.

I believe that by the last page, you'll be able to understand and converse with almost any dog on the planet.

Are you ready?

1

Dog Language

Dog language is an ancient language that's so much older than our own. How incredible to think that it's still instinctively used by every single dog on the planet today — you could say dogs have a truly international language.

More than anything, I want this book to break down the communication barriers between our two species forever. I believe it's time humans started understanding what our dogs have been trying to tell us for centuries.

In this section I'll introduce you to some fascinating dog language basics. Luckily, dog language is one of the easiest languages in the world to learn so it won't be long before you're fluently communicating with your dog as you never have before.

In dog language, your body and gestures are particularly important, so from now on I want you to be very aware of what your body language is telling your dog. Otherwise you may find your body is saying the exact opposite of your spoken words.

Chin up!

I'm curious: when I'm sitting on the couch next to Angus, my dog, he often raises his chin in an exaggerated way so that it's higher than mine. Why does he do this?

In the Dog World, a chin held high and tilted upwards means I'm more dominant than you. That means I'm the leader around here, so I'm taking control of this situation. A chin angled downwards says I'm submissive to you, so I hand you control. And a chin turned to the side: I don't want you annoying me — please leave me alone.

Next time Angus sits beside you on the couch and raises his chin above yours, understand he's telling you, Yep, I win. My chin's higher than yours, so I'm the boss of you. This is a problem, since if Angus thinks he's your boss, he won't obey you unless he feels like it.

An easy way to make sure Angus's chin always stays lower than yours is to get him sitting on the floor at your feet instead of on the couch next to you. As for your own chin, be aware of how often it's actually pointed downwards when you're around your dog. Where, for example, is it pointing when you lean down to clip on his leash?

If you want Angus to obey you, always remind yourself: Chin up!

What hugs really mean in the Dog World

Why does my dog Rosie lick my face nonstop when I hug her?

Some people are going to have a big problem with what I'm about to say but dogs really don't like being hugged. This is because in the Dog World hugs are fight-holds.

Hugging is a human way of showing affection. Dogs show affection in other ways, such as by grooming each other for ticks and fleas, or by lying companionably side by side.

So when you hug Rosie and she licks your face nonstop, she's actually asking you in the politest way she can, Please stop trying to play-fight me. You're making me feel very uncomfortable and confused. I'm submissively licking your face, begging you to stop, but you're ignoring me. Why do you keep challenging me by locking your arms around me? I really don't want to fight you — even playfully.

Rosie would prefer you to show affection in some other way. For example, you could take her for an extra walk. Or, if you're sitting calmly next to her, you could occasionally rub her behind the ears for a minute or two at a time. The more relaxed you are, the more she'll enjoy being around you. Dogs love being around calm people.

Please believe me: Rosie doesn't feel comfortable when you put one or both arms around her. Your hugs just seem as if you're forcing her into a play-fight. So don't hug your dog any more — hug a human instead!

But my dog *loves* to be hugged!

Look, I have a real problem with your suggestion that my dog Barney doesn't like being hugged. I know he loves it! Why else would he lean so affectionately against me and place his paw on my arm while I'm hugging him? Sometimes during the hug he gets really affectionate and mouths my hands and wrists playfully.

I know it's hard to turn everything you've ever thought about hugging dogs on its head but I assure you it's true: dogs really don't like being hugged.

When you hug Barney he believes you're tossing a direct challenge at him by placing your arm around him in a loose fight-hold. So he responds by throwing three challenges back at you: leaning his weight on you, resting a paw dominantly on you, and mouthing your hands and wrists in warning — these are all very powerful challenges he's now winning against you. This is Barney deliberately dominating you; he is not showing you affection.

As you can see, if you hug a naturally challenging dog like Barney he'll quickly slide into a very defiant mood. For every challenge you throw at him he's ready and willing to throw back even more at you. He's even ready to use aggression if he needs to.

For example, if you tighten both your arms around him, he may even end your open challenge by giving you a hard nip to remind you he's actually winning more challenges than you are. So please respect your dog's personal space and don't force any more hugs on Barney. Unfortunately, human hugs get too many dogs into trouble.

Tail talk

Can you explain what my dog Danny is trying to tell me with his tail?

The position in which you hold your tail is very important in the Dog World. A tail held low says I'm being submissive to you. A tail held high says I'm more dominant than you.

Get into the habit of looking at Danny's tail to see what kind of mood he's in. If you see his tail go up, take control before he starts misbehaving. A low tail means your dog is willingly giving you respect, so you'll know Danny's accepting your leadership.

What's in a yawn?

Can you tell me what my dog Snoopy is saying when he yawns?

Yawns can mean more than just tiredness to a dog. When Snoopy yawns with his chin held really high, he's saying, Relax everyone, I'm the boss around here and I'm taking control of this situation. A yawn to the side means I'm in a relaxed mood — why aren't you? Go away and relax too.

A yawn with his chin tucked in downwards to the side says, Please don't get aggressive with me. I'm being submissive to you but you're not accepting my apology. Now you're getting me confused. What else can I do to stop you getting angry at me?

If Snoopy's feeling very confused, he'll follow this yawn with a head or body shake. This is his way of trying to rid himself of his tension. If you see these signals, it's time to calm your body language down and start giving Snoopy clearer commands, because confused dogs are unhappy dogs.

I want you to start using yawns as a way of communicating with your dog. For instance, if there's a problem in your household and Snoopy starts getting stressed and asking for your help — perhaps by barking and running around — raise your chin and yawn slowly. Your slow, sleepy yawns let Snoopy know he can relax because you're now taking control.

Of course, this means you do have to get up and sort out the problem that's stressing your dog. Remember, Snoopy will only believe your leader's yawn if you prove you do sort out all problems straightaway.

On the other hand, if Snoopy's annoying you for more attention, raise your chin, turn your head away and yawn sleepily. This tells him to walk away and relax somewhere else. It's much more effective than shouting at him or trying to push him away from you, because when you're yawning, you're also calming him down.

Remember, calm dogs quickly stop misbehaving, so whenever your dog is misbehaving do everything you can to calm him down as soon as possible. Yawning with your chin raised is a very powerful way of doing this.

Please don't feel silly when you yawn at your dog — rather, exaggerate your powerful yawning signals. Believe me, Snoopy will know exactly what you're saying.

Am I boring her?

What does it mean when I hear my dog Zoe yawn loudly?

Dogs yawn loudly as a way of asking for your help. When Zoe does this, she's saying to you, Hey, are you there, Boss? I really need your help right now!

For example, Zoe might yawn if a child is acting around

her in a way that's making her feel nervous and stressed. A loud yawn is her polite way of asking you to take the child away. Or she might be gently reminding you that you haven't walked her yet and it's getting dark. Or perhaps she's letting you know she's accidently been locked outside, and you haven't realised it yet.

Loud yawns are much more submissive way of asking for your help than barking. It's a dog's way of drawing the leader's attention to a problem without being demanding.

In future, I suggest you work out what Zoe's loudly yawning about, because it might be something important. If you ignore her loud yawns, Zoe will be forced to fix the problem some other way — perhaps by noisily barking to get your attention or, worse, by nipping that bothersome child.

Blinking Bug

Sometimes I notice my dog Bug blinking frequently at me. Is he trying to tell me something when he does this?

Blinking can indicate how relaxed or nervous a dog is. Occasional slow blinking means Bug feels nice and relaxed. Fast blinking means he's feeling nervous. Constant slow blinking tells you he's trying to relax you because you look stressed.

Now you have another way to calm Bug down if he gets stressed: all you have to do is deliberately slow down your own blinking so you look nice and sleepy.

Don't stare at Bug when you're trying to settle him down; instead, raise your chin and look away sleepily into the distance, blinking slowly and throwing in a few slow, relaxing yawns for good measure.

You'll be amazed at how powerful this slow, sleepy blinking is in the Dog World. It will help relax even the most anxious, stressed dog.

Licking lips

Why does my small dog Emily lick her lips constantly when I cuddle her?

Just like humans, dogs lick their lips a lot when they're nervous, and many dogs, especially small dogs, will lick their lips nervously when their humans try to cuddle them. This is because cuddles, just like hugs, are seen as challenging fight-holds in the Dog World.

If Emily's licking her lips nervously while you cuddle her, then she's desperately trying to tell you how much she doesn't want to play-fight with you, so please listen to what she's saying and stop cuddling her.

Any other time you see Emily nervously licking her lips — for example, if a stranger bends down to pat her — prove you're a good leader by helping her solve her problem. In this case, you might politely explain to the stranger that your dog is nervous of people she doesn't know, but that they can relax her by yawning away from her instead.

You'll be a much better leader if you learn to spot when Emily needs your help. If she's licking her lips, she's asking you to help her solve a problem. So if you want to be a great leader for Emily, help her solve her problems.

Jump-up Jilly

Why does my dog Jilly love to jump up on me when I get home from work? Is she just excited to see me?

Every time Jilly jumps up and plants her paws on you, she's saying, I just marked you dominantly with my scent pads — now I'm your boss. The more Jilly jumps up on you, the more she proves her point.

As jumping up on humans is such a dominant challenge, I want you to develop zero tolerance to her doing it to anyone ever again. The more aloofly you act, the less she'll want to challenge your authority. So raise your chin nice and high and have a distant expression on your face as you get out of your car. Ignore Jilly completely as you walk towards your front door.

Don't look at her, pat her or talk to her. If she happens to get in your way, raise your chin even higher and simply barge straight through Jilly as though she's not there. If she tries to jump up on you, raise your chin even higher, fold your arms and again barge through her as you head purposefully for the front door. Show how confident you are by not hesitating. Act calm but aloof, as though nothing unusual is happening at all. Now you're acting like a true leader in the Dog World!

Once you reach your front door, turn around and walk straight back to your car in the same way. Walk back and forth to your car until Jilly is no longer tempted to jump up. After a week of being barged through every time she attempts to jump up on you, she'll realise you're no longer going to accept being rudely dominated by her. She'll test you occasionally for a few more weeks, but when she keeps meeting your no-nonsense reaction, she'll eventually give up.

As she starts behaving more respectfully — for example, standing calmly out of your way, looking up at you and wagging her tail in the polite low position — you can stop ignoring her so much. Don't make a fuss of her, just say a calm 'Hello, Jilly', as you walk briskly past her. From now on, I suggest you put off touching your dog for about ten minutes after you arrive home. This will keep your homecomings calm and respectful.

If Jilly tries to jump up on anyone else, raise your chin, fold your arms and barge through her in the same way as before, so she's forced to step back out of their personal space. (Never let children or other adults barge through Jilly, as most dogs won't accept this.) From now on, your dog needs to respect the personal space of all humans. The new rule is no more jumping up on humans, Jilly.

I'm not sure I like the idea of barging

In the last solution you suggested barging through a dog when it gets in the way or jumps up. But won't this hurt my darling little dog Sally?

This is not a cruel idea of mine; it's simply part of the language that dogs use with each other all the time. Leader dogs will always barge through followers who insolently get in their way. Barging is accepted practice in the Dog World and all dogs know it means I'm the boss, so get out of my way quick smart!

Don't be fooled: although you may think Sally just innocently happens to stand in your way, she knows exactly what she's doing. You'll find submissive dogs will naturally move out of your path. Only dominant personalities will linger stubbornly to test your leadership.

As Sally sees you coming she knows what to do: move. By standing her ground she's deliberately trying to block your way so you will submissively detour around her. She's even prepared to get barged a few times in the process. Very dominant dogs don't mind getting hurt if they get a chance to win a challenge. That's what dominance is — the willingness to do anything to win the leadership.

You won't need to barge Sally for very long, just until she learns to step politely out of your way. If she acts like a drama queen when you barge through her, ignore her — just as any leader dog would. She's attempting to get you fussing submissively over her. Soft-hearted dog-owners will find their dogs try this on because the owners have always fallen for their dog's theatrics before. But after a week or so Sally will automatically melt out of your way.

As the leader, you should never find your way blocked by a dog. Remember: if Sally tries to stand in your way, simply barge through her. This will help her decide if her rude challenge is worth it.

When *shouldn't* I barge through my dog?

My dog Wilma growled at me when I barged through her for standing in my way. What should I do now?

Wilma growled at you in warning to tell you, Grrrr ... don't you dare act as though you're my leader. I've won so many challenges against you in the past that I'm now your boss. If you ever do anything that disrespectful to me again I'll nip you.

I want you to treat any aggression Wilma shows towards you, such as growling, as a very serious offence. But don't hit or yell at her. Instead, be very aloof with Wilma until she starts treating you with more respect. Don't feed her that evening's meal so she's reminded why you should be her boss — because you provide her precious food. One missed meal is not going to kill your dog, however, she will become more submissive.

I want you to be very distant with her for a week. During this time, don't look at her more than can be helped, try not to talk to her and definitely withhold all affection from her. Continue to walk and feed her, of course, but give her no attention at all — pretend she doesn't exist. Now you're acting like Wilma's leader, not her follower.

The next time she blocks your way, stand still, raise your chin and send her away while saying curtly, 'Go away! Go!' Never chase or hit her — and don't try to drag her out of your way by the collar.

There are many solutions in this book that suggest you barge through your dog just like any good leader in the Dog World would. However, I don't want you barging through Wilma again until she stops showing any sort of dominance towards you. You may never be able to barge through a dominant personality like Wilma if you feel unsafe doing so.

I also suggest you read through this book several times before you try out any of the other solutions on your dog. This book is full of great ideas about how to make yourself the leader of your dog, but some extremely dominant dogs are willing to fight very hard to hang onto their leadership.

I always want you to take your safety — and that of your family — seriously. Never use a solution from this book if you think Wilma is going to be aggressive towards you. Please use your common sense so you don't get bitten.

Stop taking those Submissive Steps

Is my dog Fred stupid? Whenever I call him to me, he comes most of the way over, then stops. When I try to call him the rest of the way, he just ignores me and keeps standing there until I give in and walk over to him. What's this all about?

Fred certainly isn't stupid. In the Dog World, if you can stand still and lure others into walking all the way over to you, then you win.

Let's see how this challenge works. If Fred is walking towards you, then stops and waits for you to come to him, he'll watch you walk the rest of the way and he'll think, Yep! I've tricked you into taking a few Submissive Steps over to me, so that means I win; I just proved I'm more dominant than you.

Every single step Fred can trick you into taking towards him while he stands still makes him feel more dominant — especially those last few very important steps.

21

From now on, simply stop taking any more Submissive Steps towards him. However, if Fred's won this challenge many times in the past, you're going to have to get clever about persuading him to walk all the way over to you. If you do find yourself in a Mexican stand-off with Fred, don't get angry; instead, become ingenious.

Try bending down and swaying from side to side as you tap your hands on the ground in front of you. In dog language this says Come and play with me. It will take a very strong-willed dog not to come straight to you when you do this. As Fred reaches you, raise your chin and stand up to regain control and stop him from feeling playful.

If Fred's feeling extremely stubborn, you can move even further away from him and, with your back turned to him, pretend to suddenly discover something on the ground that's exciting or really delicious to eat. Pantomime catching it in your cupped hands and he'll walk right up to you to investigate. The more theatrical you are, the more curious he'll be.

Now you understand how Submissive Steps work I want you to become really aware of those moments when Fred casually lures you into taking them. They can be surprisingly easy to miss. For example, say Fred has fetched a ball, but instead of dropping it at your feet, he stops a metre away, inviting you to take two or three steps over to him to pick it up. Please don't fall for Fred's trick: make him come all the way to you. Another time, you might call Fred to have his leash clipped on, and he stops short, inviting you to take that last half-step to reach his collar. Again, don't fall for this trick!

Remember, if you take even half a step towards Fred while he's standing still, it's a Submissive Step, so keep your eyes open and always get Fred to come all the way to you.

Now you know the truth: in the Dog World, leaders never walk submissively over to anyone.

The powerful chest

I've heard you say on the radio that you shouldn't pat your dog on the chest — but I have to say my male dog Paddy absolutely loves it. Why is it such a problem?

Every time you pat Paddy on this powerful spot you'll find he begins to lift his chin higher and his chest will puff out more. What he's saying is, Yes, keep on patting me submissively in that exact spot. You're putting me in a very powerful, dominant mood because patting me there reminds me of how it feels to mate with a female. No wonder Paddy loves it: pats on the chest really get his adrenaline pumping!

My advice is to refrain from patting any dog on the chest, throat or belly, or under the chin, especially male dogs. It's one of the fastest ways to hand over control to them. So pat Paddy only on the areas of his body that will make you more dominant, such as on the top of his head, on the back of his neck and on his shoulders.

From now on, make sure you don't give Paddy the wrong message: no more submissive pats.

Why Wally wants a pat

When I visit my friend's house, I always give her dog Wally a pat so he'll go away and leave me alone. Why, then, does he keep on annoying me?

Wally really wants you to pat him as soon as you arrive. That first pat you give him instantly makes you submissive to him. Now he can throw lots of other annoying challenges at you.

In the future, don't submissively pat Wally. In fact, I want you to calmly ignore him for the entire visit.

Whatever you do, don't give Wally that first submissive pat or you'll open the floodgates and bring a stream of endless, annoying dog challenges upon yourself — and get Wally into trouble as well.

Who do *you* greet first in the morning?

I love saying good morning to my beautiful dog Orlando. He's always so happy to see me, but I have a question for you: why does he never come to me first thing in the morning? I find he stands and waits stubbornly for me to walk over and give him a pat. My kids say he does this to them, too.

In the Dog World, the leader stands and waits first thing in the morning until everyone in the pack comes over and submissively greets him. By waiting for the pack to do this, the leader gets the chance to see who's in a challenging mood. For example, who's dragging their feet about coming over to pay homage to him — or who's testing his leadership by not coming over at all. Obviously, because he's the one waiting for you all to walk to him, Orlando sees himself as the leader of your pack.

The solution is easy. From now on, greet all the humans in your household before you greet Orlando in the morning. Even if he tries to grab your attention away from the humans, simply raise your chin and ignore him until you've greeted everyone else first.

If you're the only human awake, ignore Orlando until he comes over to greet you. If he tries luring you over to pat him by standing still and waiting, don't fall for his tricks! Crouch down and call him to you by swaying from side to side and tapping your hands on the floor. As he approaches, raise your chin and stand up. Now you can give him a calm morning greeting by rubbing him behind the ears. Whatever you do, don't take any Submissive Steps towards Orlando first thing in the morning.

Now Orlando knows who's leader of your pack before breakfast: you!

The Circle of Power

My dog Cooper runs up to me whenever he wants and licks me, sits on me and leans against me. How can I get him to respect my personal space?

The truth is, if Cooper doesn't respect your personal space, then he'll never respect you enough to let you be his leader. Let's change Cooper's attitude right now: I want you to create a Circle of Power around yourself and carry it with you forever. In the Dog World, all great leaders treat this

Circle of Power as a very important, precious thing. Dogs who keep invading it without permission are quickly treated to a sharp attack.

To create the Circle of Power, use your imagination to draw an invisible circle on the ground around you. Make this imaginary circle an arm's length away from you in all directions. From now on, adopt this simple rule: Cooper is not allowed inside your Circle of Power unless you give him clear permission to enter.

To get Cooper to accept this invisible line, raise your chin as he approaches you so he's reminded that you're the leader, then turn your head away to deny him entry. Tell Cooper to sit when he nearly reaches your invisible line. Once he's calmly sitting, tell him to stay. Make him wait politely at the edge of your Circle of Power by holding out your hand like a traffic cop while keeping your chin raised and your head slightly turned away.

Once Cooper is showing submissive signals, such as lowering his ears and his head, and being politely still and quiet, you can say, 'Come!' as you tap the ground or your thigh. This tap is your new way of giving Cooper permission to enter the inner sanctum of your Circle of Power. If you don't tap the ground or your thigh, he's not allowed to enter the circle.

Cooper should always treat the space inside your circle very respectfully. He can sit or stand while he's inside it, but his tail, ears and head should be nice and low. Under no circumstances can he run around inside the circle or jump up on you, lean against you, lick you, whine or bark, step on your toes or raise his chin insolently high. All dogs know instinctively that it's a privilege to be allowed inside the leader's circle, so if Cooper's acting rudely while he's so close to you, he's openly challenging your authority.

From now on, treat any insolent behaviour inside your Circle of Power as a very serious offence and always deal with it immediately.

The best punishment is to order Cooper sternly out of your circle by raising your chin, pointing away and saying curtly, 'Go away! Go!'

If he insolently refuses to leave, raise your chin and walk through him as though he's invisible. Cooper will quickly learn to move back out of the way of your feet. Keep walking through him until he walks submissively away and leaves you the victorious owner of your personal space again.

Believe me, you won't get a polite dog until you create this Circle of Power around yourself. All dogs instantly recognise a good leader who protects their Circle of Power. The more you treat this invisible circle as a precious space that must be respected, the more powerful it becomes. You'll be amazed at what a difference it'll make in Cooper's behaviour.

After a few weeks, Cooper will naturally be polite around you. He'll pause at the edge of your circle and will wait until you give him permission to enter by tapping the ground or your thigh. He'll stop behaving rudely near you.

To be honest, without your leader's Circle of Power, you're powerless.

Buddy's foot fetish

My dog Buddy parks himself on my feet any opportunity he gets. What do you suggest I do?

27

In the Dog World, sitting on someone's feet is an extremely dominant gesture — it's a way of openly stealing someone's personal space. The next time Buddy does this, instantly shuffle your feet forwards into him to reclaim your personal space. I call this manoeuvre the Harlem Shuffle.

As you do it, pretend nothing unusual is happening. Don't look at him; raise your chin, fold your arms and give a big leisurely yawn. This is telling him in the calmest possible way, No more stealing my personal space; respect me as your leader.

No matter how Buddy yelps or jumps up, disregard his offended act, raise your chin even higher and completely ignore him. Looking and sounding injured is a tactic dogs commonly use to get their owners looking down submissively at them and calling them back for a reassuring pat. Please don't reward Buddy's dominant behaviour with a pat.

If Buddy ignores your Harlem Shuffle, stand up, raise your chin and march through him as if he doesn't exist. He'll quickly learn you're serious about stopping him from invading your personal space.

If Buddy sits on your visitors' or children's feet, go over to him and without hesitation march straight through him with your chin raised, pretending nothing unusual is happening. As you rescue his latest sat-upon victim, ask them, too, to pretend nothing unusual is happening. The best thing they can do is raise their chin and not look at Buddy at all.

Put a stop to Buddy rudely sitting on your feet. Remember that in the Dog World, if you're sitting on it, then you're telling everyone you own it.

Leaning Lenny

My dog Lenny is so lazy! He leans on me constantly — or is this just his way of showing me affection?

Lenny certainly isn't showing how much he likes you. Leaning against you is actually a very subtle way of stealing your personal space.

As he leans on you, Lenny thinks, Aah, look at me as I slowly and gently steal your personal space away from you. Aah, this is SUCH a relaxing way to win a challenge from you … why, sometimes you even rub my ears affectionately as I'm stealing your space bit by bit from right under your nose!

To stop Lenny dominating you in this way, next time he tries to lean against you, firmly move him off by shuffling your legs forwards while you raise your chin up nice and high. Act aloof, as though he's not even there. Whatever you do, don't move backwards; always move forwards into Lenny so he's forced to move and give back your personal space.

Don't get into any arguments over this; instead, pretend he's not there and calmly take back the personal space that's yours — plus a little bit extra. Yawn slowly to show you're taking over like a calm, confident leader.

Avoid using your hands to push your dog away, as Lenny will simply enjoy your invitation to challenge, pushing back and mouthing and nipping your hands. Once you've used your legs to shuffle Lenny off, fold your arms, raise your chin and look away. This clearly tells him, Respect me!

Act more aloofly around Lenny if he keeps trying to lean on you. If he's in a particularly challenging mood, send him away from you angrily. Raise your chin and say, 'Go away! Go!'

Ignore him for a while and only let him back when he's being more respectful towards you. As he realises you now protect your personal space as a precious thing, he'll stop leaning on you.

Keep in mind one of the mottos of the Dog World: 'If you're leaning on it, you're stealing it.'

The pat pesterer

My dog Ruby has one really annoying habit: she's always bugging me for more pats. Of course I like patting her, but not when she's being pushy like this.

You have every right to be annoyed. Demanding pats from others is extremely bad manners in the Dog World. No lead dog would ever accept this behaviour from a lower-ranking dog, so you shouldn't either.

Dogs can't just barge inside the leader's personal space without being invited — and for good reason. The leader needs everyone else in the pack to be able to read what his posture, ears and tail are saying. So deliberately crowding into the leader's personal space is a direct challenge to his authority.

When Ruby crowds into your space demanding a pat, she's telling you, Yep, every time I invade your personal space and get you to obediently pat me, I prove that I'm the real leader around here, not you.

Of course, I'm not saying Ruby can't get any pats from you, but from now on, she gets zero pats if she demands them.

The idea is to completely ignore her every time she comes in close to you, rudely insisting you pat her. I don't care how affectionate she looks — no more pats if she demands them.

If she does rudely demand a pat from you, lift your chin up high, fold your arms and turn your head away in disgust. This tells her clearly, This rude, intrusive behaviour isn't acceptable, so go away.

When Ruby obediently walks away, don't confuse her by talking to her in a reassuring way or patting her rump affectionately. If you act in a friendly way to her while she's walking away, you're actually inviting her back to play with you.

From now on, when you send a dog away from you always act aloof, with your chin raised. This is how a lead dog would behave. Acting aloof means I'm serious now; I'm the boss around here, so respect me.

When you send Ruby away, she'll probably walk some distance from you and lie down with her bottom to you, giving a noisy sigh as she lays her chin flat on the floor. Don't worry; she's not sulking. She's telling you politely in dog language, Okay, you've successfully stopped me from dominating you. You sent me away to put me in my place. Now look at how nicely submissive I'm being. The best way you can appreciate her good manners is to leave her settled for a while.

From now on, Ruby, no more pats on demand.

Stepping on toes

Our big dog Barney is so clumsy: he's always stepping on our toes. Am I being paranoid, or is it deliberate?

Barney certainly isn't being clumsy. In the Dog World, if you can step on someone's toes, then you've won a powerful challenge against them.

As Barney steps on your toes, he thinks, I wanted to test if I could dominate you by invading your personal space — and, yep, you're subserviently letting me get away with it! You're clearly not leader material so I'd better take over.

The next time Barney tries to step on you, raise your chin high, fold your arms, put an aloof expression on your face and march straight through him. Most importantly, act as though nothing unusual is happening. Pretend there's no dog around you at all.

I want you to ignore him even if he yelps or leaps out of your way in a panic. Yes, perhaps he got hurt, but he's also bluffing. He knows from experience that if he sounds hurt enough, you'll immediately bend down and start fussing submissively over him. But think about it: Barney didn't mind stepping on your toes, did he?

After you've marched through him and he's learned to step back smartly out of your way to show his new subservience to you, I want you to keep on ignoring him. Act relaxed and nonchalant, as though nothing unusual just happened.

It's this casual manner that will impress Barney as nothing else will: only a supremely confident leader would have the confidence to act in such a way. It shows challenging Barney that he's having about as much impact on you, the leader, as a tiny flea — perhaps even less.

To be a great leader, I want you to ignore Barney completely as you march through him with your chin raised. Whatever you do, don't watch him submissively. After you've walked through him, pretending he doesn't exist, Barney will probably shake himself to rid himself of his confusion. He'll ask himself, What the hell just went on there?

Now he'll want to watch you closely. Dogs are fascinated by impressive leaders; they want to learn how you're winning their respect so easily. However, we don't want Barney watching us — we want him switched off and relaxing, so raise your chin, turn your head away from him, yawn slowly and blink sleepily. When you relax a dog, you quickly lull him out of his challenging mood. This is another trick gifted dog leaders use — and one you can adopt too.

In the future, you can also march through Barney with your chin raised if he tries to step on anyone else's toes. But make sure you're the one doing the marching. Most dogs won't accept children or visitors dominantly marching through them, and we don't want anyone getting nipped.

After a few weeks of occasionally testing you, Barney's toe-stepping challenges will melt away. He was just testing you to see how much personal space he could steal away from you by stepping on your toes.

Well, from now on he's definitely not going to get away with stepping on any human toes. Dogs know to the millimetre how close they are to anyone's feet, so don't be fooled. There is absolutely no accidental clumsiness in the

Dog World: any apparent clumsiness is very deliberate and should be dealt with.

Passionate Pasha

My dog Pasha licks my hands, face, feet and even my legs any opportunity she gets. I don't mind the odd lick but this is incessant. Please rescue me from being licked nonstop like a lollipop!

Pasha's licking may seem very affectionate but the reality is that she's using licking as a way of dominating you. She's invading your personal space by making you feel uncomfortable.

The most likely reason for this behaviour is that Pasha feels uncomfortable and stressed about something and she wants you to spot the problem and fix it. So look around and work out why she's feeling stressed.

Is there any disorganisation or chaos in your home? For example, overexcited or stressed visitors, other family dogs acting in an insolent way, or your children misbehaving and pestering Pasha. Another source of stress could be emotional tension in the household. For example, if you are feeling unusually stressed, or if you and your partner are feeling tense with each other.

Any of these factors might trigger Pasha's manic licking, so look around, identify what's causing her to get stressed, and fix it.

Pasha, like all dogs, just wants calm law and order around her. In her opinion something's desperately out of control, so as the leader it's your job to bring peace and serenity to the situation. Remember, the more she's licking you, the more she believes things are sliding out of control. It's up to you to work out what the problem is and solve it as quickly as possible.

As you fix the problem, you can reduce Pasha's stress by giving her plenty of relaxing sleepy signals, such as turning your head away, yawning and slowly blinking. If you can relax Pasha, she'll stop feeling so frantic.

You also have to break her nervous licking habit. From now on, if Pasha starts licking you agitatedly, fold your arms and raise your chin as you look away. This tells her, Stop trying to dominate me and go away.

If she continues to lick you, growl sternly at her. If she ignores this warning it's time to have a Stop Licking Me lesson.

Clip Pasha on a leash and secure her next to a comfortable chair. Sit back and relax as you keep holding out your hand to her. Don't stare at her, just gaze into middle distance and just let your hand drop within Pasha's reach as though by accident. Growl angrily at her whenever she licks your hand and say curtly, 'Leave it!'

If Pasha stops licking your hand, reward her by turning your head away and yawning sleepily.

Repeat as often as you need to. Eventually you will be able hold your hand out and, instead of trying to lick you, Pasha will turn her head politely away.

When you can hold your hand around her face and body and she still keeps her head turned away from you, then you know she respects you and you can release her from the leash.

Make sure Pasha doesn't try to dominate anyone else with that nonstop licking, especially your children and visitors. If you spot her licking anyone, march over to her immediately and growl down at her severely as you barge her out of her victim's personal space. Keep walking into Pasha until she retreats out of everyone's way. If she won't stop the licking, clip her on a secured leash out of the way until she calms down.

As the leader, it's your job to keep your household calm and organised. But no matter what's going on, Pasha must learn to keep that dominating little tongue to herself.

Why does my dog always lie across doorways?

Why does my dog Max never get out of my way when I walk through doorways? Sometimes I step over him, but it gets very irritating when I'm carrying the shopping inside and he won't budge. Any suggestions?

Max has found the perfect way to control you — by controlling your movements through the doorways of your inner den. Doorways are very important strategic places that dogs love to win ownership of. And all Max has to do to own a doorway is lie across it.

By not getting out of your way, Max is telling you, Yeah, you want to get past? Too bad; I'm not budging. Now you'll have to go to the trouble of stepping over me. I'm far too important to move out of the way for a mere follower like you.

Here's how we deal with an open challenge like this.

With your chin in the air, give a slow, powerful leader's yawn as you walk right through Max. Say nothing and pretend he doesn't even exist. Ignore any sudden yelps or exaggeratedly frightened leaps out of the way. When he does this, he's trying to bluff you into subserviently leaning down and fussing over him. Don't fall for his tricks by reaching down and patting or soothing him — or even looking at him. The best thing you can do as you walk right through him is to simply act as though nothing unusual is happening at all.

Never forget that, as the leader, you always have right of way. This is one of the most basic rules of the Dog World. If you don't insist that Max respects your right of way, then he'll simply assume that you don't want the job of being the leader.

March straight through Max as many times as you need to. Don't worry; it won't take him long to get your clear message: I'm the leader around here, so get out of my way quick smart or get trodden on.

Max, I'm glad to say your days of being the rebellious doorman are over.

Does your dog ever stand in your way?

I often wonder why my dog Lug is constantly getting in my way, making me walk around him.

If your dog ever blocks your way and doesn't move, then it's definitely deliberate. Lug is saying, I'm the leader around here, so detour submissively around me.

What can you do about it? Barge through him without hesitation so he's forced to move out of your way. As you do so, fold your arms, raise your chin high and don't talk to him. In fact, pretend he's not there at all. Ignore any sudden movements and yelps; he knows what to do — just get out of your way.

Lug will probably test you for a week or so, but just keep barging briskly through him every time you find him blocking your way. Don't weaken: don't walk around him, try to shoo him gently, drag him out of your way or step subserviently over him.

The rules of the Dog World are simple: you're the leader, so you always have the right of way. If Lug is insolent enough to stand in your way then he's going to get trodden on. He knows that — he's just testing you to see if you'll carry through with it.

The power of *not* looking

I heard you say on the radio that one of the easiest ways you can help your dog stop misbehaving is simply to stop watching it all the time. I have a dog called Doris that I love very much — won't it be cruel if I stop looking at her?

I'm not asking you to never look at your dog; I'm just suggesting you watch Doris much less. If you constantly watch her, then you're actually switching her on — making her feel as if she has to do something.

Doris, like any dog, won't be able to stop reacting to your gaze. She may think you're calling her over to you, so she'll come over and bug you for pats; or that you're challenging her to play a game, so she'll bounce over and start playing roughly with you. If you're watching her all the time, she may even think that you're asking her to be your boss. That's when she starts ignoring your commands. Watching dogs too much gets them into trouble.

I want you to learn that one of the most powerful ways you can calm Doris down when she's misbehaving is simply to lift your chin and turn your head away from her. Now you're not looking at her.

If you continue watching her as she misbehaves, then you're telling her, That's okay, Doris, you keep on doing whatever you want. Don't worry, I'm not going to stop you. No wonder she thinks you're asking her to be your boss!

If you do need to look at her, be more casual. Let your eyes sweep over her and move on. This is how dogs look at each other when they want the situation to remain relaxed.

Why won't he look at us?

William, our dog, has this horrible habit of sticking his nose in the air and ignoring everyone. He's such a handsome dog, we can't help looking at him all the time, but we joke that he thinks he's too good for us. How can we make him more respectful towards us?

When William lifts his nose in the air, he's thinking, When I sit here with my chin up high, ignoring everyone, I soon get everyone submissively staring at me. Sometimes I can even lure them into taking Submissive Steps over to me. This is great because they end up patting me submissively — especially on my very important, puffed out chest. Yep, if I sit here long enough, I get all the humans treating me like I'm the boss.

I find the dogs that use this attention-seeking technique are usually very handsome dogs, such as Afghans, used to having the whole family gazing in wonder at them all the time.

The way to prevent such dominant behaviour is to get everyone to ignore William until he starts acting in a much more respectful manner towards humans. This could take hours or it could take weeks — it all depends on how dominant a dog he is.

In the meantime, act aloofly with your chin raised high if you need to deal with him, for example, when you take him for a walk. Also, make sure you're not taking any Submissive Steps towards him or patting him if he's being aloof. In fact, if William starts sitting somewhere conspicuous, raising his chin and ignoring everyone, I'd march over there and barge through him so he moves submissively out of your way and wanders off to a less noticeable place.

Once William is your follower, not your leader, you can gradually give him more attention. However, the moment he starts raising his chin and ignoring you, stop giving him admiring attention.

I find dogs like William sometimes need to switch off all visual contact with people, so respect his wish to look away from everyone. However, watch out if his chin starts to rise — it's a warning sign that he's beginning to feel far too dominant again.

Why the hell do you keep staring at me?

My dog Cowboy is so handsome I can't help watching and admiring him. But whenever I watch him, he bounces straight over, demanding my attention. Why?

In the Dog World, if you look intently at another dog you're saying, Hey you! Come over here!

Luckily, this is an easy problem to fix: simply stop staring at Cowboy. Instead, learn to observe him more discreetly by letting your eyes drift over him and on to other things. If he catches you staring just raise your chin, yawn slowly, blink sleepily, and turn your head away until he relaxes.

Like any good leader, you need to learn the skill of watching your dog discreetly. Don't let Cowboy catch you in the act of staring at him any longer.

Remove those troublesome batteries!

I've decided to keep my male dog Bob's testicles intact because I believe a dog's not a real dog without them. What's your opinion?

If Bob isn't desexed he's going to be a headache to own. He'll play far more power games with you and he'll be totally distracted by sex. Those testicles of Bob's are like two powerful little batteries, constantly giving him extra energy to pour into challenging you for the leadership.

Undesexed male dogs scent-mark more, they want to roam more, they tend to be pushier and more challenging, and they can usually find ways of escaping to seek out any bitch on heat nearby.

Also, so many unwanted puppies are euthanised because they can't find homes. Don't let Bob's occasional escapes to a bitch on heat add to those unnecessary puppy deaths.

It's so much easier and more enjoyable to own a desexed dog. My advice is to desex Bob as soon as possible.

Dogs thrive on routine

I heard you say on the radio that all dogs should have a daily routine to become better behaved, but won't my energetic dog Flynn get bored by the same old routine?

Flynn will thrive on the same routine every day. Dogs don't find routine boring — they find it reassuring. Flynn, like all dogs, believes if you know what to expect every day, then you can relax!

On the other hand, any change in their routine makes a dog want to challenge you more. Every time there's a new situation, Flynn automatically has to work out who's in control. He'll do this by throwing challenges at you.

So the kindest thing you can do for any dog is to establish a simple routine you can stick to every day. The highlight of this routine is always the walk, so don't leave it out. Even better, make it two walks a day.

You'll be surprised at how much Flynn enjoys doing the same things at the same time every day. Soon you and Flynn will move through each day smoothly and easily. You'll find his behaviour and manners improve dramatically.

It quickly becomes obvious how much dogs love routine because if you do happen to make any changes, just watch Flynn protest!

Is my dog sulking?

I've noticed something odd about my dog Jack. After I've patted him for a while, he walks away to a corner of the room and lies down with his bottom to me and his chin on the floor. Is he sulking? Is he ignoring me? What's going on?

When Jack does this, he's telling you politely, I've had enough attention now; I just want to switch off and be left alone for a while, please.

He's showing you clear respect by placing his chin on the floor. He's sitting with his bottom to you, facing another direction so he doesn't keep getting 'switched on' by your movements. This is how dogs politely ask for some private time.

Now it's your turn to be polite by respecting Jack's desire for privacy and leaving him to relax in peace.

I don't want to be the leader!

To be honest, I don't really like the idea of being more dominant than my dog Sheba. She's such a gentle, friendly dog that I want us to be equals. Don't you have any alternative ideas for Sheba and me?

Sorry, but there are no alternatives to being a leader for your dog. The basic law of the Dog World is unbreakable: you can only be a leader or a follower, never equals. This is because there is no such thing as equality in the Dog World — or in the rest of the animal world. And it isn't possible to teach Sheba how to be your equal. Her brain isn't designed to understand a complicated human concept like equality, or to comprehend being treated this way. If you act as though you're Sheba's equal, she will just see you as an extremely weak leader — or as her follower.

Perhaps you're worried that if you become Sheba's leader she'll stop loving you. Actually, the opposite is true: dogs are naturally drawn to good leaders who constantly take control. This is because they feel so safe around them. And as Sheba's leader, it doesn't follow that you have to be mean to her. You can still give her affection, attention and treats. But you can never give Sheba so many of these that she feels more important than you.

So how much is too much affection and attention? Luckily for us, the rules of the Dog World are beautifully clear. You — the leader — must get everything first, as well as the most of everything and the best of everything.

However, these special privileges come at a price. As the leader you're always in charge. Sheba, on the other hand, has no worries. She simply has to be a follower — and sit back and enjoy her carefree life.

If you decide to ignore everything I've just said and continue treating Sheba as your equal, you will only confuse and stress her. I cannot emphasise this enough: Sheba will see your attempts to treat her as an equal as being incredibly weak and bewildering. One of the main ways humans stress dogs every day is by not acting like good leaders.

So I hope you take the time to read through the rest of this book and become a great boss that Sheba can trust and rely on. She'll be so much happier and she'll no longer be constantly confused. Please believe me, there really is no such thing as equality in the Dog World.

Puck's palace revolution

My dog Puck's behaviour has dramatically improved since I started following your suggestions. However, last weekend we had friends stay with us and now Puck's back to his old naughty ways. What on earth happened?

When you had visitors to stay, Puck found hundreds of opportunities to win challenges against them, and with all his victories, his sense of self-importance swelled. As a result, he's misbehaving again just as he used to.

As Puck sees it: If I managed to get away with winning all those victories from those pesky visitors in just a few days, then maybe I should try challenging my way up to the leadership job again. How about I test everyone in the family again and see how I score this time? Maybe I'm more of a leader than I thought.

It's time to stop Puck's little palace revolution. A weekend orgy of scoring victories against visitors doesn't make him your leader. Remind him of this fact by taking away all his freedom for a few days until his dominant mood subsides. For example, put Puck in his pen when he's outside. Clip him on his leash mat when you invite him inside. Keep him on his leash when you take him out in public.

I also want you to be more aloof with Puck until he's behaving more respectfully. So raise your chin nice and high when you're around him, and reduce the amount of time you look at him, touch him and talk to him. While he's on his leash, get him to submissively come to you and sit constantly on your command. All of these steps will make him feel much more submissive and it won't be long before Puck's pretensions to rule fade — perhaps a week or so.

A word of advice: next time you have visitors stay for the weekend, keep Puck on his leash or in his pen, and ask your friends to ignore him. Don't let a weekend visit become the beginning of another climb to power. Visitors staying overnight can make dogs feel very ambitious!

Send him away

When I find my dog Bill doing something wrong I angrily call him to me to reprimand him. But he runs away and hides. This just gets me angrier with him. Shouldn't he have to come to me when I tell him to?

It's not Bill's fault he won't come near you when you're angry. In the Dog World, if another dog's angry at you it's actually very challenging to go anywhere near it until it calms down.

Bill's worrying that you'll attack him if he does come to you! He's getting confused because he's wondering why you're calling him. He knows you should be sending him away from you if you're angry.

Once you calm down, then he'll respectfully come to you after a while, exaggerating his submissive behaviour so you don't hurt him. All dogs do this to show the leader they accept his authority again.

So when you next get angry with Bill, understand that

it's natural for him to walk away and lie low until you've calmed down again. This is his polite, subservient way of showing he's now trying to do the right thing for you.

In future, if he does something seriously wrong, send him away from you instead — then go and cool your temper down. When Bill returns to you later, be very aloof around him.

If you want, you can win a few simple challenges against him by clipping his leash on him and getting him to submissively obey the three powerful commands 'Come', 'Sit' and Stay'. If you want to punish him further, ask him to do these commands a few more times. Winning some challenges like these is a much better way of putting yourself back in control than smacking and yelling at your dog.

If you find you're getting angry with Bill for misbehaving in a place where you can't send him away — say, if you're down at the park — control your temper, crouch down low and call him to you in a happy, calm voice. Now clip him back on his leash and simply act in an aloof manner and ignore him for the rest of the afternoon. Withdraw all affection and attention from him until he acts in a more respectful way to you.

Losing your temper is not good leader behaviour. In fact, it usually makes dogs misbehave even more because they can see you've lost control.

Become inexhaustible, not angry

When my dog Darrel keeps misbehaving, I get so frustrated I smack him — but even this doesn't make him behave. If anything, he only gets naughtier. What else can I do?

Instead of getting angry when Darrel tests you by misbehaving, learn to get calmer. If Darrel sees you losing your cool, he thinks, Wow! Look how freaked out my human's getting. He's obviously not capable of dealing with this problem, so I'd better start taking over. He'll do this by misbehaving even more.

Darrel's also learned to let you exhaust yourself with anger and then, when you're too tired to argue with him any more, he simply does his own thing anyway.

I suggest you learn to stay calm no matter what Darrel does. Instead of getting angry, simply clip him on a leash and secure it to something fixed, so he can't escape, then walk away and ignore him. This is one of the best ways you can slide a naughty dog back into a more submissive, obedient mood.

In the Dog World, leaders use their sharp teeth to forcibly settle down pushy dogs that won't stop misbehaving but, as you're a human leader, you can clip Darrel on a leash instead. This is a much kinder way to discipline your dog.

Some people mistakenly think the tougher you are with your dog, the more he'll respect you. However, dogs aren't impressed by how angry you get, how loudly you scream or how hard your smacks are. Dogs only respect leaders who stay calm, relaxed, clever and inexhaustible no matter what happens.

Darrel has to learn that, if it takes ten, a hundred or even a thousand times, you're always going to calmly make him do what you want. In time he'll learn you never give up, so why waste energy arguing with you?

Learn the power of the leader's growl

What's the best way to reprimand my dog Duke if he needs it? He usually does what I want, but sometimes he ignores me when I ask him to stop annoying me. For instance, what can I do when he won't stop annoying me for pats even after I tried your suggestion of acting aloof.

A lead dog can quickly stop a troublemaker dog from annoying him simply by issuing a low growl. The softer the growl, the more powerful the boss dog is seen to be. Once you're Duke's established leader, you have earned the right to growl at him if he won't stop doing something disrespectful.

For example, you might use the leader's growl in the scenario you've mentioned, when Duke won't stop bugging you for pats and you've already asked him to politely stop by raising your chin, folding your arms and turning your head away.

The leader's growl sends your dog an unmistakable message: Stop disrespecting me immediately! It's a much more powerful way of reprimanding Duke than smacking him.

To do the leader's growl, raise your chin and tilt your head so you're glaring down at Duke from the corner of your eye. Now go very still and give a deep, warning growl. You'll sound even more impressive if you place your tongue on the roof of your mouth.

The leader's growl is serious business and all dogs know exactly what it means. However, whether Duke respects you enough to obey the growl is another matter. A dog only respects you when he stops what he's doing the moment he hears your leader's growl.

If Duke doesn't stop what he's doing immediately, then you're going to have to work on becoming a better leader who has more authority over him. The leader's growl is an excellent way to quickly reprimand your dog, but you must earn the right to use it first. The solutions in this book will help you win more respect from him.

However — and this is very important — always remember that the leader's growl is only to be used by the leader. By this, I mean an adult who's usually in charge of Duke. Don't let young children, teenagers or visitors ever use the leader's growl on your dog.

Please, never take the leader's growl lightly. It's a very serious action to take in the Dog World, so don't underestimate, misuse or abuse its power.

My leader's growl didn't work

I growled at Duke because he wouldn't stop bugging me for pats, but he just ignored me. What do I do now?

If Duke ignores your growl he's openly defying your leadership and there are three things you can do about it.

If your dog isn't aggressive towards you, you can raise your chin and march straight into his personal space as you growl again at him. With every step he submissively takes backwards from you, you earn the right to be in charge and have your leader's growl obeyed.

The second way you can respond if Duke ignores your growl is to immediately take away his freedom. Clip him on a leash and secure it to something fixed, such as a verandah railing, a sturdy hook in the wall or a post. Raise your chin and growl while looking down at him from the corner of your eye, then walk away. This tells him: Watch how easily I can put you in your place when you ignore me. Learn to respect my growl.

Why clip your dog on a leash like this? In the Dog World, lead dogs force troublemakers to stay submissively in one spot until they learn to respect their authority. Securing Duke on a leash so he has to stay in one spot is much kinder than forcing him to stay in place by attacking him with sharp teeth every time he tries to move away!

The third option is to banish Duke from your presence. If Duke completely ignores your growl, send him away from you angrily. Raise your chin and glare at him in disgust, saying, 'Go away! Go!'

He can wander off to a corner of your backyard and think about things for a while on his own.

Being banished from the inner den (the inside of your house) and everyone else is a very serious punishment in the Dog World, as dogs are naturally sociable and hate being separated from the pack.

When you send him away, ignore Duke completely as though he doesn't exist. He'll return to you eventually in a more respectful manner, but ignore him for a while longer, and be very aloof around him for the rest of the day.

It's important to get Duke respecting and obeying your leader's growl. Although it's only a verbal warning, it's a very powerful way of reminding your dog instantly of your authority.

Once Duke respects your leader's growl, you'll be able to stop any of his rude, challenging behaviour straightaway. The more he respects you, the softer your growls can be — and the faster he'll stop disrespecting you.

Aggro from Angelina

My dog Angelina became aggressive when I used the leader's growl on her because she wouldn't get off my bed when I told her to. What should I do now?

Treat any aggression your dog gives you as an extremely serious offence. Don't touch her, but stand tall and stiff and send her away with a stern, 'Go! Go away!'

She'll slink off, so let her go away to think over what just happened. Leave her alone and act very aloofly towards her for the rest of the day. Don't feed her that night (one night won't kill her). Every dog should learn: never bite the hand that feeds you.

Now you need to work out why she felt she had the right to growl at you. She's obviously winning some important challenges from you at the moment — for a start, she's dominantly getting up on your powerful leader's bed. I suggest you read this book through several times before you try growling at her again.

However, if in the future Angelina's aggression gets worse when you growl at her it would indicate that she's unwilling to let you be her boss, and that is an unacceptable attitude for any dog to have. In such a case I believe she may be too risky to own.

Think about it: if she's always a hair's-breadth away from nipping you — the person who actually feeds her — then this dog is unsafe around all humans.

I believe unsafe dogs should be euthanised. One of my favourite mottos is 'The safety of humans always comes first'.

Don't show weakness

Am I being paranoid? My female dog Graffi seems to misbehave even more than usual when I'm injured or sick, or if I'm feeling tired or distracted. What do you think?

You're not being paranoid. Graffi, like all dogs, will instinctively test your leadership the moment she senses you're not feeling focused, observant and strong-willed.

Dogs are predators, so they're extremely talented at spotting vulnerability in another animal. As soon as Graffi sees you're under the weather, then that little survival voice inside her head says, Oh no! My human obviously feels weak today; I'd better take over the leadership job straightaway! Quick — start throwing challenges at him!

This means that even at your weakest, you can't let Graffi throw challenges at you.

The easiest way you can do this is to restrict your dog's freedom more on those days you don't feel at your best. That way she'll have fewer opportunities to challenge you.

For example, you might put Graffi in her dog pen (see 'Welcome to Dog Land', pages 101–2) with a bone when she's outside during the day. Clip her on a leash mat when you bring her inside of an evening. Don't let her off the leash when out on walks.

No matter how ill you feel, try not to let Graffi use your sick days as opportunities to do whatever she likes, otherwise you're going to have win back all those challenges at a later date. Believe me, it's so much easier to avoid losing challenges to your dog in the first place.

You'll find the more dominant Graffi is, the more she'll want to take over the leadership when she spots any weakness in you. Don't take it personally — Graffi's just programmed by Mother Nature to automatically take over when her leader looks weak. This is an issue of survival in the Dog World, not disloyalty.

My dog won't sit for me

My dog Rebel hates sitting for me. Why's he so stubborn about this one thing? And how can I teach him to do it?

Rebel doesn't want to sit for you because it's a very submissive thing to do. He obviously thinks he's more important than you, so it's definitely time to change Rebel's rebellious attitude.

Clip Rebel on his leash so he's immediately in a more submissive frame of mind. Hold the leash firmly so he can't retreat backwards. As you confidently step towards him with your chin raised, use the leash to pull his chin straight up in the air. With nowhere to go, he'll sit back on his haunches as you walk the last step towards him. As soon as he sits, say, 'Sit. Good boy.' Now you can step backwards from him after you've firmly commanded him to 'Stay'.

Although you're taking Submissive Steps towards him, his sitting for you is even more submissive, so don't worry; you're still in charge.

Practice this until Rebel obeys on the command 'Sit'. If he tries to test you by hesitating, raise your chin higher and step towards him so he sees you mean business — and he'll sit.

Food treats as a teaching aid

Can I use food treats to teach my dog Molly to sit for me?

Sure. Have Molly hungry for her first training session. Clip on her leash so you put her in a much more submissive mood straightaway.

Now let her smell the bag of special treats you've prepared. If you want to be extremely persuasive, organise a bag of cooked chicken, fried in garlic and chopped up small with all the bones removed. Treats like this really remind Molly why you should be her leader — because you provide the precious food!

She should be salivating at the delicious smells wafting from your bag by now. Raise your chin and calmly say, 'Sit', as you hold up a small bit of chicken. When she sits, I want you to pretend to nibble the treat first, then drop it on the ground at her feet as you say, 'Sit. Good girl.'

If Molly won't sit and just stares up at you, help her focus by folding your arms and turning your back on her. Wait a moment, then turn back and try again. Continue until she sits politely for you.

If Molly stubbornly refuses, don't take any Submissive Steps towards her; instead, taking a few steps backwards, pull the leash and say, 'Come.' If you keep getting Molly to come to you, then you'll lull her naturally into a more submissive frame of mind. When she's respectfully coming to you, try commanding her to sit again.

Raise your chin and turn your back on her until she decides that yummy treat is worth more than dominantly refusing to sit. (This is why I suggested you have her hungry for the lesson.)

Once she's sitting well for you on the leash, practice getting her to sit for you off the leash. Again, don't be tempted to take any Submissive Steps towards her.

Now practice until she sits for you no matter where you are, whether she's on a leash or not, and no matter what distractions are going on around her.

You'll know when Molly respects you totally as her leader, because she'll sit instantly at your feet every single time you calmly say 'Sit'.

Fire your boss at feeding time

My dog Horse is really pushy when I feed him. We leave dry food in a bowl for him to pick at all day so he can't possibly be hungry, yet at dinnertime he acts like a starved maniac! He jumps around barking noisily and barges around my legs. This is getting really annoying. What do you suggest I do?

In the Dog World, whoever controls the food, controls the pack. If Horse is acting in a pushy, demanding way around food, then he's openly trying to grab the leadership from you. As he barges around you at feeding time, he's telling you, Hurry up! I'm the boss of you, so I demand you feed me RIGHT NOW! So hurry up! Faster! FASTER!

The solution? From today, have two new food rules for Horse: always feed him last and don't give him any freedom while he eats.

Here's the simple routine I use to teach pushy dogs manners at dinnertime: before Horse gets fed, clip him on a secured leash. Now — and this is very important — get him to sit for you. You're reminding him: I supply the food, therefore I've earned the right to be the boss of you. Show me I'm the boss by sitting subserviently at my feet.

Before you put Horse's food dish down, pretend to nibble at it, then make a disgusted face and say, 'Yuk!', then drop the dish at his feet and leave to let him eat in peace and privacy. This easy piece of play-acting tells Horse he isn't demanding this precious food, you're just giving him your unwanted leftovers.

While he's eating, don't stare at Horse, as this is an extremely rude in the Dog World, and don't tease him by constantly taking his bowl away while he's eating. Some people mistakenly think this is a way to prove who's the boss of the food, but your dog will simply learn not to trust you. Powerful leaders always treat food as a very serious matter that deserves respect.

Following this simple feeding routine will send Horse a very powerful message that you control the food now, not him. After a while, you won't need to clip him on his leash. He'll just sit politely at your feet to get fed.

Finally, let me say a word about leaving out a bowl of dry food for Horse to pick at all day: if food is the money of the Dog World, then you're leaving an open wallet around so Horse can help himself to it whenever he feels like it. I suggest you stop leaving out dry food for Horse to pick at or he'll feel far too much like the boss. (Don't worry, Horse isn't going to starve between meals; dogs don't need to have access to food all day.)

To me, dinnertime is the biggest lesson of the day for all dogs. It's the one undisputable moment when Horse remembers exactly why you should be the boss — because you always provide his precious food.

Does free food fall constantly from your fingers?

I can't help myself; when my dog Teddy stares up at me with those big, pleading eyes while I'm eating, I always weaken and share some with her. I've heard you say this is bad for her, but she doesn't have a weight problem. Why should I stop?

When dogs stare at you for food tidbits, they're not pleading, they're demanding. Even the softest, cutest eyes are telling you in silent dog language, I order you to give me that piece of food RIGHT NOW!

As you can imagine, this is not a great habit to teach Teddy. She'll quickly believe she's your boss if you keep obediently handing her your food on demand.

Dogs simply don't understand the human idea of sharing food — especially delicious treats. In the Dog World, sharing precious food with someone who isn't your own offspring isn't seen as a sign of kindness, generosity or love; in your dog's eyes it's just weakness. As Teddy sees it, if you didn't want the food, you'd just walk away and leave the leftovers on the ground for her.

Food is so important in the Dog World, don't weaken your power over it by submissively handing it to Teddy every time she demands it. Think about it: at the moment all she has to do is look at you — and you obediently feed her!

In future, if you want to give Teddy a treat, make sure she does something for you first. For example, ask her to 'Come' and 'Sit' for you. These are submissive actions she can perform to earn your food reward.

To remind her that she's not forcing you to hand over this bit of food, always get into the habit of pretending to nibble the treat first, then saying, 'Yuk!', and dropping it at her feet. Now she'll think that this bit of dropped food is simply your unwanted leftovers. This little piece of play-acting will make you seem even more powerful in her eyes.

Food is the money of the Dog World, so from now on never give it away for nothing.

What's wrong with watching my dog eat?

I love watching my dog Pig eat — he really tucks into his food and gobbles it down just like his namesake. However, lately he's started growling at me when I watch him. Shouldn't I have the right to watch him eat if I'm the leader?

Pig believes you're carefully watching him because you're looking for a chance to grab back his food and eat it yourself. That's the only reason anyone intently watches someone else eat in the Dog World. Staring at Pig while he eats is extremely bad manners and I suggest you stop it immediately.

There's a much better way to feed Pig his evening meal. From now on, clip him on a leash in his usual feeding area. Get him to sit submissively for you. Pretend to nibble at his food, then make a face and say, 'Yuk! That's disgusting!', then drop the bowl down on the floor at his feet. Now walk away with your chin held high to leave him eat in peace.

Now Pig's got absolutely no reason to growl at you. The message you're now giving him is, I provide the food, not you, so I'm the leader. You can have this food I no longer want, but you must sit for it. I can be trusted to be your leader because once I feed you, I always let you enjoy your food in peace.

Bon appétit, Pig!

Bones, beautiful bones!

Can you tell me what you think about bones? One vet I saw recently tried to get me to buy some synthetic chew products for my dog Barnaby. He said they were necessary for his teeth.

I'm a huge believer in giving dogs a raw bone every day. Dogs are designed to chew bones — but make sure you only ever give raw bones, as cooked bones are dangerous for dogs.

Raw bones have so many benefits for dogs. They're the natural toothbrushes of the Dog World. They're also a natural way dogs can chew off their stress. Chewing bones also burns up spare energy. They help to relieve the discomfort of growing teeth. They help soothe pups or anxious dogs left home alone. They help relax a nervous dog (as long as they are left undisturbed). They help dogs digest their other food. Most of all, they're packed full of healthy vitamins and minerals that are so good for dogs.

I love to see a dog that's just returned home, pleasantly tired out by a walk, go and settle down to chew a lovely raw bone. Now that's a contented dog. All you have to remember is not to watch your dog while it chews a bone, as this is very challenging, bad manners in the Dog World.

Here's the best way to give Barnaby a bone. Ask him to sit for you. Pretend to nibble the bone, then pull a disgusted face and say, 'Yuk!' Now drop the bone at Barnaby's feet and walk away to leave him to chew his bone in peace. If you have another dog, clip them both on leashes so they can't squabble.

What can I say? I just love recommending raw bones for dogs!

Dogs don't want to be instant friends

The other day I saw a dog waiting outside a shop for his owner, but when I leaned down to pat him in a friendly way, he growled at me. Why did he do this?

The trouble with humans is that we want to be instant friends with dogs — even if we've never met them before. However, it's extremely bad manners in the Dog World to rush up to a strange dog and move straight into its personal space, staring at it and trying to touch it. This sort of behaviour is very confrontational for most dogs.

I want you to try to imagine how dogs must feel when they're tied up in a public place. There you are, standing on the pavement minding your own business and feeling extremely vulnerable because you're trapped by that leash, when a gigantic human stranger suddenly walks directly towards you, moves in scarily close, looms over you, and starts ruffling your hair and sticking their face right in yours. I guarantee you'd feel very uncomfortable, even scared.

The best thing you can do when you see a dog tied up down the street is leave it alone. If you must interact with it, do this: as you casually pass by at a very polite distance, turn your head away while slowly yawning and sleepily blinking — and keep on walking, leaving it in peace. It will most probably ignore you, so please respect its desire to be left alone.

Dogs find it very stressful being tied up in public, so please don't add to their stress.

Greeting a dog you don't know

Martin, I'm curious: how do *you* normally greet a strange dog who's with his owner and on a leash?

Simple — I pretend the dog doesn't exist! I pay attention only to the person holding the leash as we have a conversation. This clearly shows the dog he's not important enough to be noticed. By ignoring the dog, I'm telling him he's of no interest to me, so he should relax and switch off.

When I say I ignore the dog, I mean I don't look at him,

talk to him or try to touch him. Instead, I act in a very aloof manner while keeping my body language as relaxed as possible. I fold my arms, raise my chin and turn my head away, all the while yawning slowly and blinking sleepily.

If the dog is acting in a very aloof way to me, then he's politely asking me to leave him alone — and I do. However, if he's a very pushy dog, he might throw a few challenges at me. For example, he might lean against my legs, try to nudge me for a pat or even jump up on me. If he tries, again I simply fold my arms, raise my chin nice and high, and turn away from him as though he doesn't exist.

If I keep slowly yawning and sleepily blinking he'll soon lie down and snooze on the end of his owner's leash. This is the best way to relax a pushy dog on a leash — make him sleepy!

These are all great ways to show a strange dog you're a very dominant leader worth respecting. It's worth doing: if a strange dog respects you, he'll politely stay out of your personal space and won't annoy you.

As you become more fluent in Dog Language, you won't feel the need to touch strange dogs as much as you used to. You'll be able to communicate in a doglike way rather than a human way.

Picasso's selective hearing

Why does my male dog Picasso sometimes obey my commands, but at other times completely ignore me?

There are two possible reasons. Firstly, Picasso might be ignoring you as a way of saying, I can hear your command but I don't feel very submissive to you right now, so I'm not going to obey you.

This is a cheeky challenge to your authority and I suggest you immediately move Picasso from his rebellious little spot by barging through him while repeating your command. If he still doesn't obey you, clip him on a leash and calmly get him to do what you want.

Picasso has to learn that you're not issuing a command just to hear the sound of your own voice. Teach him to respect your commands by making him do as you ask. If he absolutely refuses to obey you, don't get into a pointless fight; just get him doing something submissive for you, even if it means clipping on his leash and making him obey the simple command 'Come!', by tapping the ground in front of you.

However, Picasso could have another reason for ignoring you — he might be very confused. If he's confused, then he's not naughtily ignoring you. Rather, he's switching his ears off to shut out any more stimuli because his brain is already overloaded with information.

Contrary to what most people believe, dogs are quite simple creatures. All those clever dogs on TV and in the movies have tricked us into believing dogs are much more intelligent than they really are. The truth is, dogs can easily become confused when they find themselves doing something unfamiliar.

You can tell if your dog is confused and is trying to switch off his hearing because he'll turn his head away from you and start panting heavily. Perhaps he'll half-shut his eyes as well. This is another way he'll try to shut you out. No matter what you do, he won't look back at you.

If Picasso's this confused, then he's very stressed indeed. As his leader, it's your job to calm him down and take away his confusion. To do this, calm your own breathing down and relax yourself. Now raise your chin to show him you're taking back control. He may shake off his stress and wander off to relax by himself.

If you're in a place where you have to restrain Picasso, clip him on a leash and either hold the leash or secure it so he can't walk off. Now just ignore him until he settles down. Give him some relaxing yawns and sleepily blink, but don't look at him for a while. This will give him time to calm down and stop feeling so overwhelmed and confused.

Then you can take Picasso for a walk. A brisk walk is a great way to soothe a dog's nerves and help it get rid of its stress. Watch as Picasso gratefully shakes off his stress!

The nose knows

Can my dog Olaf tell how I feel?

Yes, your dog sure can. Olaf can tell whether you're feeling happy, relaxed, sad, frightened, excited, confused, aroused, stressed or angry from the pheromones your body releases.

Every emotion you feel automatically sets off a chemical reaction in your body and, as a result, unique pheromones are released from your skin, glands and orifices every time you feel a different emotion. Your dog's highly developed sense of smell can detect these pheromones on your skin and clothing, and in the air around you. This is why dogs constantly sniff each other, and us: to work out how everyone's really feeling.

If you see Olaf sneeze during one of these delicate sniffs, he's trying to clear out any distracting scent molecules trapped in his nose. Once his nose is clear he can better decipher the scents coming from you.

Sometimes your emotions are so strong they are easier to read, as many more pheromones are released. No wonder your dog knows you so well!

The scent of confidence

How can I smell more confident if I see a scary dog approaching Olaf and me when we're out on a walk?

Say you're walking Olaf down the street on a leash when a big, scary dog approaches you. Of course you know how to act: like a confident leader. So you raise your chin and try to look relaxed as you give Olaf the firm command to 'Leave it!' However, you know very well you must smell scared.

What happens next is that Olaf sniffs the air near you and thinks, Nope, I'm not obeying your command to leave that dog alone. You smell really frightened, so there's no way I can leave you in charge. I have to take over and scare that dog away from us before he smells your fear too! So … WOOF! WOOF! WOOF! Get away from us, you big, strange dog! Forget how scared my human smells because I'm in charge now and you don't scare me!

The solution is to work out some simple action you can take to make yourself feel — and therefore smell — more confident. For example, you could say to yourself, Do you know what? I'm going to ignore that scary-looking dog and cross this road with Olaf. While I'm crossing the road I'm going to raise my chin and yawn very confidently.

It doesn't matter exactly what you decide to do, as long as it's something so simple that you can do it with complete confidence. As you carry through your simple plan, your scent will become more confident, too.

Olaf will smell the change in you and think, Okay ... I can still smell the fear coming from you, but I can also smell that new, more confident smell you're giving off too. Yeah ... there's enough confidence in that mix for me to give you a chance to stay in charge.

Now Olaf will be less likely to take over and launch an attack on the other dog.

Aah, the difference your smell can make to your dog's behaviour! If you smell more confident, then Olaf will be more likely to obey you, especially in a time of crisis.

Are you freaking out, trying to win every single dog challenge against your dog?

I'm starting to think I'm going crazy. Ever since you pointed out all the challenges my dog Stevie's been winning, I've become a bit manic about trying to win them all. Now he seems to be challenging me more than ever. Please help!

Stevie's deliberately throwing as many petty challenges at you as he can. He wants to fluster you — and it sounds like his plan is working! Stevie's hoping you'll think winning challenges is just too hard and exhausting. He wants you to give up. The solution? Stop trying to win every single dog challenge — especially the petty ones. Save your energy for winning the important ones.

The important challenges are anything to do with aggression, children, visitors, noise and your personal space when you're trying to ignore your dog. Always do something about these challenges.

Any other sort of challenge — well, just see how you feel at the time. If you're too exhausted to deal with anything petty just raise your chin like a leader dog and pretend you didn't see it. This is a trick I learned from some extremely wise dogs!

The best idea is to create a calm daily routine for Stevie, and gradually work on getting it problem-free over a period of time. Your dog is going to be alive for a long time, so treat challenges as a long-term project. If it takes you three weeks or three months to get a respectful, well-mannered dog, so be it. Don't expect to win all the challenges overnight.

Believe me, when Stevie sees this new attitude in you, he'll be impressed. He'll quickly stop throwing challenges at you all the time and make you his boss. Staying determined over time isn't glamorous but in the Dog World, it works.

Why does my champion obedience dog challenge me in public?

My dog Tybolt is a well-known champion obedience dog but sometimes he embarrasses me between classes when we're not in the show ring. For example, he sometimes pulls on the leash when he knows very well not to. Other times he drags me over to something on the ground and sniffs it. Meanwhile, people are watching us, smirking. He never does this at home! Why does he want to publicly embarrass me on show days?

I believe Tybolt's still a little tense after strutting his stuff in the show ring. I have a saying: if tension goes into your dog it has to escape out somehow. These small misdemeanors between classes are simply his tension escaping in small, silly ways.

Dog show rings are places swirling with tension, emotion and stress — and Tybolt needs to release the stress he's picked up inside the ring somehow. He may try shaking it off as he leaves the ring, but if that doesn't work he might try to release it by tossing you a few petty challenges.

If you were at home you'd deal with these in your usual capable way, but because you have a very judgmental audience watching you at the showground you tense up. The more you tense up, the more Tybolt misbehaves.

Without realising it, you've started an anxious cycle that won't end until Tybolt finds a natural release for all that tension building up inside him. The solution? Relax more. Forget what other people think.

The next time Tybolt throws you a petty challenge after a class, forget your audience and deal with it as you normally would at home. If he still disobeys you, say to yourself, 'So what?'

The best way to release Tybolt's stress is to take him off for a brisk walk away from the crowds and other competitors. After a while your walk will become calmer as you both rid yourself of your stress.

Dancing with dogs

I've started going to a dog-dancing club with my gorgeous big dog George. But I'm starting to feel rather silly because George refuses to get up on his hind legs and dance with me. All the other dogs in the class seem to love it. What's wrong with George?

Congratulations, you have a real gentleman of a dog! In the Dog World, jumping up on someone is a classic way of trying to dominate them. This means George, by refusing to dance with you, is actually refusing to challenge you in a rude, dominant way. I really admire mannerly dogs like this.

How does George really see your dance class? To dogs, human dancing is exactly like a mock-fighting game. Think about it: imagine if you were a dog. Then you and George would be two dogs facing each other on your hind legs, with your front paws up high on each other, staring straight into each other's eyes. This is one of the ways dogs fight.

When the music stops, and your class of dancing dogs drops back to the ground, I bet there are a lot of dogs shaking their heads and bodies. Dogs try to shake off their stress in this way when they're confused and stressed.

I also bet there are a lot of nervous, heavy panting and manic, overexcited dogs after the class. And I wonder how many dogs try to mouth and nip their humans when they get too overexcited by being in a fight-hold for long periods of time.

I do admire your George, however. When you tried to force him into play-fighting along with you, he politely refused your challenge by dropping submissively back down. When you kept trying to force him to dance, he politely tried to walk away.

I have to be honest: I'm really against the idea of dancing with dogs. It sends dogs the wrong message. When you say, 'Shall we dance?', your dog gets the message, Shall we play-fight?

Naturally dominant dogs are encouraged to be even more dominant around humans. More submissive dogs, like George, just become very confused and stressed.

If you want to dance, I suggest you join a human dance class. This would be much kinder for your gentleman George than forcing him to mock-fight with you against his will. It's cruel to force dogs into doing things that confuse and stress them, especially when they've already politely tried to refuse your invitation.

Panting to tell you ...

My dog Jen pants a lot when visitors play with her. Why does she pant so much? Is she excited or is she just overheating?

Dogs aren't always happy when they pant. Heavy panting can tell you that your dog is getting very anxious. Like Jen, some dogs get quite stressed by visitors — after all, visitors are intruders in a dog's territory. As Jen runs around desperately trying to win as many challenges as she can from the intruders, she can feel the pressure mounting. All the time she's thinking, Am I controlling everyone successfully? Why do all these pesky humans keep trying to dominate me by putting their paws on my head? And if they're trying to dominate me, why are they giving me so many subservient signals, such as patting me under the chin or on my chest? Oh dear ... human visitors confuse me so much!

Most dogs find humans bewildering because we act in subservient ways, then dominant ways, then subservient ways again — sometimes within the space of a few minutes. This means Jen can never stop challenging your visitors until she works out exactly who's in control.

Heavy panting is a sure sign that your dog is feeling very stressed. A good leader is an observant leader who always steps in and fixes the problem, so learn to spot when your dog's feeling stressed and immediately work out a solution. In Jen's case, you can help take the pressure off her by asking your visitors to completely ignore her and pretend she's not there.

High anxiety

I have a real problem with my dear little dog, Ellie. When she's in my arms and someone tries to touch her she shivers, then all of a sudden strikes out and nips them. If I smack her nose, and tell her to stop being so silly, she simply growls. She just can't be patted by anyone except me when she's up in my arms. What's she thinking?

When Ellie's high up in your arms and another person walks over to you and tries to pat her, she thinks, Hey! How DARE you try to touch me! I may be shivering because I'm scared, but I'm also very important — can't you see how high my human is holding me? Grrrr! Go away! Don't touch me!

Ellie believes she can growl at anyone who tries to touch her because you're holding her up high. Little dogs feel incredibly dominant when they're lifted up in your arms. So keep Ellie down on the ground on a leash where she won't feel so important — especially if you're near another person.

If you must pick her up for some reason, make her do something for you first, such as obeying your commands to 'Come' and 'Sit'. This will make her feel much less dominant.

When you're talking to another person and Ellie's at your feet, clip her on a leash. Small dogs find strangers especially scary, so Ellie will find it much less stressful if they leave her alone. Explain this to the other person and ask them not to stare at Ellie or touch her as it makes her very nervous and aggressive. In fact, the best thing they can do is completely ignore her.

If someone is talking to you and Ellie starts looking stressed, you can give her some relaxing signals, such as raising your chin and, without looking at her, yawning slowly and blinking sleepily. Keep your chin raised high to show Ellie you're in complete control of the situation. Toss her a treat every now and again to distract her.

Now she'll stop thinking, Oh no, here's another annoying, scary stranger I'd better keep an eye on. Instead, she'll simply think, Oh goody, another stranger means another treat ... YUM!

Oops! Is that your ego getting in the way?

Why does my usually well-behaved dog Johnson only seem to misbehave when my friends come over? I want to impress them but instead they keep seeing a really badly behaved dog that won't stop bugging me for pats. The other day when my friends came over, I got so frustrated and embarrassed by Johnson's behaviour I ended up yelling at him. But instead of settling down, he just ran around the yard barking noisily. Why won't he stop trying to humiliate me when my friends are watching?

The reason Johnson misbehaves in front of your friends is because you worry more about what your friends think than what Johnson's thinking.

As you tense up, worrying whether Johnson is going to disobey you in front of your friends, your dog automatically senses you're feeling weak. This is why he starts bugging you for pats. He doesn't do this because he's naughty, but because he's stressed by your sudden, tense mood. Basically, as you tense up, he'll come over to you looking for reassurance.

The more everyone stares at Johnson — no doubt enjoying secret little chuckles at your embarrassment — the more you tense up. This only makes Johnson more stressed. This is why his behaviour just keeps getting worse until he ends up racing around, barking noisily. Some dogs run around barking as a way of trying to rid themselves of too much stress.

The next time your friends come over, throw away your ego! Believe me, your fragile human ego is only going to weaken your leadership because it makes you care too much about what other humans think. It causes usually smart humans to act in un-smart ways. From now on, if your dog makes a mistake in front of an audience, learn to shrug it off and think, So what?

If you want your dog to see you as the leader, then the

most powerful thing you can do is to completely relax. Think about it. Only leaders who have incredible confidence can remain calm in front of a watching audience. So ignore the human smirks around you. Slow your breathing right down, raise your chin, slowly yawn and sleepily blink. Shrug off your embarrassment. Now you're back in control, behaving like a true dog leader for Johnson.

So forget impressing your friends. Instead, stick to impressing Johnson with your awesome calm leadership that can't be flustered by anyone or anything. If you act like a true dog leader your dog will automatically be well behaved for you. If you work on impressing Johnson, then your friends will be impressed by the way he responds for you.

Do you watch your dog too much?

My husband and I love watching our little dog Bim as she races around amusing us all day with her funny, crazy antics. However, I've noticed she gets very naughty if we watch her too much — and sometimes she really exhausts herself. But after a brief rest she starts acting silly again. Why do you think this is?

Bim is getting extremely stressed because you won't stop watching her. This is why she constantly runs around, barking and acting silly.

Every now and then she'll go and sit down, exhausted and overwhelmed. She'll pant heavily, blink her eyes fast, or perhaps half-close her eyes to try to shut out your intense gaze. She'll scratch or chew at herself; she'll try to shake off all that nervous energy building up inside her. After a while, unable to find a release, she'll erupt into another burst of frantic behaviour.

But why is being watched all the time so stressful for her? When you stare intensely at Bim, her adrenaline kicks into action and she goes straight into overdrive, with all her natural hunting instincts firing up ready to be used if necessary. However, nothing is actually happening in your household; you just keep on relentlessly watching her for hours at a time and, try as she might, she can't switch off your gaze. The result is a dog that's fast becoming a nervous wreck. Unfortunately, the crazier she acts, the more you watch her.

So how can we bring some peace back into Bim's life? The solution is simple: stop watching her all the time. I'm not saying you can't look at her at all, just watch her much less.

I also want you to look at her more discreetly. Don't stare directly at her; instead, casually let your gaze drift over her and then on to other things. You can also change the way you look at her when you pat her. Rather than staring down at her intensely, gaze nonchalantly into the middle distance as you rub her fur for a few minutes at a time. Half-close your eyes in a sleepy way and slow your breathing right down. She'll find this much more relaxing.

If Bim starts acting in this manic way in the future, then you're probably watching her too much again. Immediately help her relax by turning your back and ignoring her. Yawn slowly and blink sleepily as though you're half-asleep.

I also suggest you and your husband find a new hobby, because if you keep watching Bim all the time, she's going to have a nervous breakdown!

Is your shy dog faking fear?

We have a very shy, nervous dog called Nutmeg that we're having some problems with. For example, most nights she's too nervous to eat, so I have to spoonfeed her dinner to her. Also, she gets too nervous outside in the dark, so I let her in to let her sleep on my bed. She shies away from other people and sometimes she even cowers around me, trembling, until I give her lots of reassurance. How do you suggest I solve her anxiety problem?

Perhaps Nutmeg had a good reason for being nervous and shy once upon a time. However, these days she's only pretending to be anxious. Why? Let's face it: when Nutmeg acts nervous and shy she ends up getting a pretty good deal from you.

Think about it: she now gets spoonfed her dinner every day like a spoilt empress. She gets to sleep on the best bed in the house. She gets you watching her submissively as you keep checking she's okay. When she cowers against you, she gets to lean on you. This is all dominant behaviour. Nutmeg's just worked out how to get away with it by seeming extremely undominant!

For example, I'm sure when she doesn't want to do something, she suddenly acts very nervously — perhaps trembling very fearfully as she cowers. I bet you usually fuss over her and let her do whatever she wants.

After all, what's a little bit of theatrical trembling if it earns you plenty of privileges?

There are probably other clues revealing how dominant Nutmeg is. Perhaps she stands in your way quite a lot, so you submissively move around her. She might lure you into taking Submissive Steps over to her as you kindly reassure her. She might also come over and nudge lots of pats from you.

Of course, when she deliberately dominates you in these gentle ways, she does it in a very shy, wide-eyed, anxious way. Please remember, I'm not saying she's a bad dog — I'm just pointing out how clever she is at winning challenges any way she can.

How do I know she's faking this anxious behaviour? A genuinely scared, anxious dog would hide all the time and try to be as submissive as possible. It wouldn't eat in front of you at all. It would sleep under your bed, not dominantly on top. It wouldn't bug you for pats and would shy away from your personal space. Believe me, Nutmeg's learned to sham anxious behaviour so she can win lots of privileges from you. She's actually quite a dominant personality.

Where did she learn to pretend to be scared? At some time in the past while she was genuinely anxious, she noticed that if she cowered, trembled and looked up at you with big, scared eyes you gave in to her immediately. She stored this useful information in her memory. Later, when she wasn't anxious at all, she tried the technique again and realised it worked wonderfully whenever she wanted to get her own way. It's a very subtle way of winning challenges against humans — and it definitely works, especially with kind, soft-hearted owners.

From now on, I suggest you ignore all Nutmeg's nervousness when she puts on her shy act. Behave as though you can't see any of her silly, anxious behaviour. If she continues to behave nervously, I want you to act in an even more aloof way. Don't give her any attention if she's faking fear. Instead, raise your chin high and completely ignore her.

You also have to do something about all the challenges she's getting away with at the moment. For example, get her tethered on her own bed in a corner of your bedroom, rather than letting her sleep dominantly on top of your bed.

Stop spoonfeeding Nutmeg her dinner. Put the meal bowl down on the ground for fifteen minutes, and pick it up again when her time is up. If she doesn't finish it — too bad. After a week or so, she'll stop trying to play dominant games with her food and just eat it. If she doesn't eat it all, you've been feeding her too much. Don't worry — dominant dogs like this never starve themselves.

Stop letting her cower against your legs. It's just a clever way of leaning dominantly against you.

Keep an eye out for all her small challenges too. Don't take any more Submissive Steps towards her to fuss over her. No more submissively looking at her all the time to check she's okay. Don't let her nudge you dominantly for any more pats. You get the idea. No dogs should win challenges against humans — it doesn't matter what kind of personality they have.

However, I do understand that new situations and strangers might genuinely make Nutmeg feel anxious. When she's genuinely scared, the best way to relax her is to simply turn your head away, yawning slowly and blinking sleepily. Stop watching her so much — and definitely stop worrying about her! Dogs naturally copy the mood of their lead dog — so if you relax — then she will too.

Please don't let Nutmeg's anxious act fool you any more. Dogs are ingenious at winning challenges any way they can — even by pretending to be nervous and helpless.

It's time to stop letting Nutmeg play you like a puppet!

Freaked out by visitors

I have an anxious dog called Angel. Even though my visitors are very loving and sweet to her, she still freaks out when they talk to her and try to pat her. What can I do to help Angel cope with my guests?

It can be very frightening for a shy dog like Angel to be touched and stared at by visitors. After all, in the Dog World visitors are seen as intruders in your territory.

The best way you can get Angel to relax around visitors is to ask your friends to totally ignore her. This will take a lot of stress off Angel. Ask your visitors not to pat her, look at her or try to talk to her. In fact, ask them to pretend she doesn't exist!

If she keeps pacing around the house in a manic way, clip her on a leash and secure it so she can't move far off the mat you give her. Place the mat in a safe place where she'll be out of the way but can still see you and reassure herself that everything's okay.

For instance, you could organise for her to occupy a corner of the living room. However, don't place her where everyone will stare at her, as this will make her feel too vulnerable. Let her have a place where she feels quite safe and hidden, such as behind your chair.

You and your friends can occasionally give Angel relaxing

signals by turning your heads away from her, raising your chins and slowly yawning and sleepily blinking.

If she still looks a bit anxious, every now and again toss her a treat, but pretend to nibble it first. Now instead of thinking, Are those intruders going to try to hurt me?, she'll just think, YUM!

It's virtually impossible to get kids to leave dogs alone — and for shy, nervous dogs like Angel, children are particularly unpredictable and scary. So if you have young, noisy children over to visit, I suggest you put Angel in a place where she'll be left alone, say in a locked pen or laundry.

In time, Angel will learn not to be so freaked out by visitors — and why not? They now only ignore her or give her relaxing signals, so she feels much safer. Angel just needs time to learn to trust human visitors.

I'm not your boyfriend!

I'm worried about my lovely little dog, Larry. I live on my own, so I got a dog for company. When I watch TV I love having him up on the couch with me. I kiss and cuddle him and hold him on my lap — but now he won't stop trying to escape from me. I'm upset: doesn't he love me any more? Why won't he show me any affection?

Congratulations, your little dog Larry isn't being unaffectionate; he's actually showing beautiful, respectful dog manners to you. When you pull him close to you, lavishing him with all that human affection, he thinks, Oh no, why does she always want to challenge me every evening on the couch? I find it so confusing! For a start, she tries to make me sit dominantly on her lap — but then she wraps her paws around me in a tight fight-hold. When I try to wriggle free she keeps me pulling me closer to her, staring intently down at me as though she's challenging me even more. Worse, she keeps pulling me close to touch her muzzle to mine. Doesn't she realise how confrontational she's being? It's as if she's demanding we start a face-to-face fight! When I lick her face submissively, begging her to stop, she just ignores me and keeps holding me tightly. I can't make my anxiety any clearer: I'm panting heavily, I'm nervously licking my lips, I'm blinking my eyes fast and I'm trying to pull away from her. What else can I do? I know ... Escape from her — ESCAPE!

By the time poor Larry jumps off the couch, he's actually done everything he can not to dominate you. He sounds a real gentleman of a little dog, though very stressed.

I bet that once Larry jumps down, he often shakes his head or body to try to rid himself of his confusion and stress, then walks away and lies down in a corner with his bottom to you and his chin flat on the floor. This is very submissive behaviour and Larry's politely asking you in dog language to leave him alone.

My advice? I want you to start becoming much more aware of what Larry's trying to tell you. For example, stop giving him all that extravagant human affection that only makes him feel very uncomfortable and confuses him.

A much better way of showing Larry affection is to ask him up onto the couch next to you. Don't lock him in a fight-hold hug or stare intently at him. Instead, just calmly raise your chin and, looking away from him, gently rub him behind the ears every now and again for a few minutes at a time.

Don't try to make him sit, lie or lean against you. Dogs prefer sitting or lying near someone they trust. They don't need to be touched; they just want to share the moment in a really relaxed way.

As for all that human affection bursting out of you, please don't waste it! Get out into the world and find someone special to give it to. You deserve to get some human love back yourself.

When Maggie's humans fight

I've noticed when my husband and I have an argument over boring bills, our dog Maggie starts really misbehaving by barking and running around the house. She also keeps stopping and sitting down to chew herself at the base of her tail. Why do you think she does this?

All dogs get extremely anxious when their humans start to fight. After all, this could be the final fight that ends the pack! When Maggie sees you both argue, she begins to panic. She thinks, Oh no, they're fighting again! Is the pack going to fall apart? I have to try to get rid of my stress by running and barking it off! Oh dear, that's not working — all this stress is making my itch start up again on the nerve endings at the base of my tail ... I'd better chew at it.

Dogs are hypersensitive to human emotions and find tension extremely stressful. Even silent, simmering human anger will set off a sensitive dog like Maggie. The solution?

Argue away from the house where Maggie can't witness it. Do what you can to have a serene, happy household.

Any sort of change is scary and stressful for dogs

I recently left my husband and moved house, and my rather shy dog Meg now seems very disturbed by all the changes. She's more anxious and hides a lot. Have you any suggestions?

Change worries dogs, but especially shy, anxious dogs like Meg. Whenever the pack breaks up or moves address, it's very stressful in the Dog World. So act very confidently around the house and adopt a no-nonsense, relaxed attitude that seems to say, Yes, this is all different, but don't be worried about it because I'm in charge.

If you act nervous, emotional or stressed around Meg, she'll become even more anxious. There's nothing more frightening for a dog than seeing a leader who doesn't seem fully in control of a new situation.

I also suggest you don't watch Meg all the time, because if you look at her constantly then it seems as though you're asking her, Well? When are you going to take over, Meg?

Instead of watching her, become more aloof and raise your chin as you walk around to show you're taking control.

To relax her, turn your head away from her and occasionally yawn slowly and blink sleepily, and generally look as tranquil as you can. This will be very reassuring for Meg because you're obviously not scared or panicking. Sleepy calmness means safety in the Dog World.

As soon as you can, I want you to establish a new routine for Meg, including two walks a day, as dogs really relax when there's a strong daily routine in their life. Routine is very reassuring in the Dog World — it means everything's back to normal.

It will also help if you give Meg a raw bone every day, as chewing bones is the natural sedative of dogs. Now Meg can chew off her stress.

However, the fastest way Meg is going to relax is by watching you relax — so start enjoying your new life!

Is this goodbye forever?

As I'm leaving for work in the morning, I try to reassure my dog Bambi by hugging her and whispering to her that I'll be back in the afternoon and everything will be okay. But every morning it's the same: she starts freaking out; trembling and wanting to follow me into the car. My neighbours have complained that she howls after I leave. How can I make these morning goodbyes less heart-rending for us both?

When you leave Bambi in the morning, Bambi thinks, Oh no! She's leaving again! Why is she acting so nervously? Look at her — she's crouching down submissively to me. Why is she staring at me in that intense way? Now she's grabbing me close and pulling me into one of those play fight-holds she calls a hug. I'm so confused and nervous: is she ever coming back? Now she's walking away, looking back at me in a stressed way. What's she so scared about? Is something bad going to happen? Oh no ... she's gone!

Now I feel more nervous than ever! COME BACK! COME BACK! Coooooooooooooooome baaaaaaaaaack, Pleeeeeee eeeeeeeeeeeeeeeeeeeeeeeeeeeeeeeeeeeeeeeeeeeeeeeeeeeeeeeeeeeeeeeeeeeeease!

To teach Bambi to feel more confident as you leave, you need to change the way you behave around her every morning.

From now on, have a different attitude and new body language. Be much more relaxed and confident. Don't look at her at all. Instead, give Bambi plenty of relaxing signals by raising your chin, yawning sleepily and looking away from her.

Create a new leaving routine. If possible take Bambi for a good, brisk walk in the morning before work; at least around the block but ideally try to give her a long, exhausting walk so all she wants to do is snooze all day.

When it's time for you to go, leave with no tension or hesitation. If you bend down and mollycoddle her, you'll seem weak and anxious in her eyes. Instead, totally ignore her anxiety as you get ready to leave.

Consider leaving Bambi in your laundry all day. If she's had enough exercise earlier, she'll just want to snooze all day anyway. Give her a few raw bones to help soothe her and keep her distracted. Chewing bones is the natural sedative of the Dog World. Put a radio on for company and to block out any scary outside noises.

As you put her inside the laundry with her bones, don't stare at her. Instead, raise your chin and yawn sleepily. Don't pat her. Definitely don't give her a hug. Don't even really look at her as you firmly say, 'Stay!', as you walk out the door.

You could even ask your vet for a sedative to help relax

her. This will help get her through the first few scary weeks while she learns she'll be safe when left at home alone.

However, the most important thing you can do to help Bambi relax is to start acting like a better leader all the time for her — not just as you're walking out the door on your way to work. This will dramatically increase her confidence. For a start, stop treating her as being more important than yourself. Stop giving her so much attention and affection all the time. Stop watching her all the time.

You'll be amazed at how much more confident she'll become. Anxious little dogs that have been forced into the role of leader become even more anxious. They just can't cope with the responsibility of being the boss. She'll feel more settled and confident when she doesn't feel like your leader.

You should also teach her to enjoy spending time on her own. When you're at home, get her used to not being around you so much. Send her away from you and out of the room you're in sometimes. Get her spending time out in the garden. If she's allowed to glue herself to your side all the time she's going to find it much harder to cope when you leave her alone.

As for those scary goodbye hugs and cuddles on your way out the door — please don't give her any more. She just thinks you're locking her into a play fight-hold on your way out!

Please cut my fringe — I can't see!

My dog Mozart is a breed that has a naturally long fringe that flops into his eyes. I think he's having trouble seeing out from under it — do you think this makes him ignore me sometimes?

I certainly do! I've learned over the years that if a dog can't see out from under his fringe he's usually less attentive.

I want you to trim Mozart's fringe as soon as possible. If you feel nervous attempting this take him to your vet, as the staff are used to doing such procedures.

Once you cut Mozart's fringe he'll see much more of the world around him. He'll be able to read your body language easily for the first time; he'll be able to read the body language of other people and dogs. I find that many dogs switch on and become much more alive when you cut their fringe. They don't look down at the ground so much and they start becoming much more attentive to you. Please help Mozart see the world beyond the boring barrier of his fringe!

Finding Dog Zen

Martin, I've heard you say on the radio that you try to find 'Dog Zen' when you spend time with dogs. What do you mean by this?

Dog Zen is that moment when there's pure, perfect communication going on between you and your dog.

Although you may be smiling at how whacky it sounds now I truly hope you get to experience Dog Zen in the future. You'll be with your dog, communicating with each other as normal but then — aah! — you unexpectedly reach an even higher level of communication where everything just works perfectly. Suddenly, you'll find you've reached an unexpected moment of pure cooperation between your minds — even though you're of different species.

For me, there's no feeling like it in the world! It's an incredibly powerful yet calm sensation — and it makes the hairs on my arms stand on end as I get a sudden rush of pure energy. Even other people and animals can feel the energy when it happens.

So read through this book and start putting these ideas borrowed from the Dog World into practice. Once you're communicating with your dog fluently — and once he accepts you as his leader completely — then one day you too may feel that wonderful, rare moment of Dog Zen.

2

The Boss of the Den

Your home territory is the main battleground where your dog is really going to try to challenge you for the right to be the boss. The inside of your home — the inner den — is an especially powerful place for your dog. This is because in the Dog World, if you win control of the den, then you also win the right to lead the pack.

However, you don't necessarily have to use aggression to win control of the den, because there are plenty of other ways a clever dog can make itself the boss of this all-important area. In this section, I'll teach you how to spot when your dog is trying to win the leadership from you inside and around your home.

Why should dogs learn to behave when they come inside?

Martin, why are you so adamant dogs should behave when they come indoors? To be honest, I don't mind if my little dog Muffy plays around when she's inside.

The inside of your house is the important 'inner den' and this is a very powerful place in the Dog World. The leader expects everyone to treat the inner den with respect. This is a place where you quietly relax and snooze, not boisterously play. If Muffy's playing noisy games inside then she's not being respectful to you.

From now on, I want you to remember that the inner den should always be treated as a sacred, serene place that is ultimately yours. It's a place where you — the leader — should always be respected by everyone.

Your new rule should be, If I allow you inside, Muffy, then you should respectfully laze around quietly in here — or get out immediately! This is what any good lead dog would insist on.

If Muffy starts disrespecting you indoors, then she should automatically lose the right to be inside — or she should be tethered on a leash so she can relax on a mat in a corner. Don't unclip her until she's treating you and your inner den with much more respect.

Curbing indoor rowdiness

My dog Sotheby is too rowdy when I bring him inside. What do you suggest I do?

Start clipping Sotheby on a secured leash in a corner of the room whenever he is inside, with his own special mat to lie down on. Although it sounds like such a simple thing to do, this method will quickly teach your dog beautiful manners inside your house. He'll learn that when he's indoors he should behave calmly and lie down and relax.

After a week or so of doing this, you can unclip Sotheby and he'll simply stay lying down on his mat.

If Sotheby does start getting rowdy again, curtly command him to 'Go to your mat!' and then clip him back on the leash. However, Sotheby's mat should be seen by him as his sanctuary, so make sure no-one bugs him when he sits on it.

This mat-and-leash method is a very gentle way of bringing law and order to your household. Lead dogs have to use their sharp teeth to teach rowdy dogs manners inside the important den area. Humans are lucky: we can use leashes and mats instead.

Before you even walk in the door, I'm planning how to dominate you

When I get home from work and put the key in the door to unlock it, I can hear my little dog Claude clawing and scrabbling boldly away at the bottom of the door. He's really damaging it. Any suggestions?

As Claude scrabbles at the bottom of your front door, he's thinking, Hurry up! Hurry up! Get this door open so I can dominate you as soon as possible! I've been waiting to do this to you all day, so hurry up and open this door!

This is why, when you open the door, Claude erupts out of it and jumps all over you, licking you, scratching you frantically and barking as he races around you. Within moments he proves he's more dominant than you.

It's time to stop Claude from feeling so dominant — or you won't have any front door left.

For a start, stop Claude feeling that he owns the inside of your house. The inner den is such an important place in the Dog World; whoever rules there generally rules the pack.

The best way to take away Claude's feeling of power in the house is to simply take away his freedom indoors until he learns to respect you.

Don't allow Claude to roam around inside your house when you go out. Build a pen with shelter in your backyard so he can stay outside in fine weather, and leave him in the garage or laundry if the weather's bad. Now he won't feel like he's the boss of the den when you're away.

When you come home, ignore Claude for a few minutes. Don't let him turn your homecoming into a chaotic shambles. By not immediately paying attention to him, you're clearly telling him he's not more important than you.

Make him sit submissively for you as you raise your chin and clip him on a leash. Now you can bring Claude calmly inside, but make sure he stays behind you as you walk through any doorways or he'll think he's more important than you again.

Tether Claude's leash in a corner of the room, give him a mat to sit on and go about your normal business, totally ignoring him. Once he's settled and calm, you can start showing him affection.

Now you're sending a clear message that tells Claude, I'm the boss inside my house, not you. He can get his indoor freedom back once he stops being so demanding and pushy, but only when you're at home.

It's time for Claude to start treating your homecomings with better manners. Once he respects you, he'll also start respecting your door.

I'll take the best bed ... of course!

Why can't my little dog Duchess sleep on my bed?

If you let Duchess sleep on your bed you're giving her the clear message that she's extremely important — even more important than you! This is one of the easiest ways little dogs win the leadership from their humans.

If you really want Duchess to sleep in your bedroom, make sure you have a separate dog bed for her down on the floor in a corner. To make sure she stays on it, clip her on a secured leash so she can't jump up on your bed.

If she protests, ignore her. Raise your chin, yawn loudly and lie down, then turn your back on her and pretend to go to sleep. Don't watch her, as she'll see that as an open challenge and start barking at you. Make sure she's been exhausted by two good walks during the day so she simply drifts straight off to sleep.

If Duchess still protests, keep your bedroom door closed at all times so she can't freely wander in and reclaim your bed when you're not watching. Be much more aloof around her until she accepts her floor bed. Increase her exercise so she's even more exhausted.

I know Duchess may protest at having her powerful bed reclaimed by you, but her days of winning this important challenge are over. There's been a revolution in the palace at last and the rightful leader is now sleeping in the royal bed — you!

TV hog

Our dog Foxy loves to join the family while we watch TV of an evening. Lately, however, she's been standing right in front of the TV, blocking our view. Every now and again, she walks around, grabbing a pat off everyone before going back to hog the TV again. What's she up to?

If everyone's looking at Foxy — even if it's only because she's standing directly in front of the TV — then she must be the most important individual in the room! She confirms this every time she walks around and demands a pat from everyone. With every pat she gets, Foxy proves she's the boss.

The solution? Teach Foxy better TV manners by tethering her on a leash in a corner of the room, with a mat to sit on, whenever you watch TV during the next week. A week spent on the leash will definitely make her feel much less important.

If you unclip Foxy and she attempts to stand in front of the TV again, send her back to her mat. If she tries it again, clip her back on her leash until she's behaving more respectfully.

If she tries to walk around demanding her royal pats again, ask everyone to raise their chins, turn their heads away, fold their arms and ignore her. If she keeps being pushy, clip her back on her leash. You'll be surprised how much a leash can settle down a demanding dog inside. This is because no freedom means no power in the Dog World.

Don't waste your time feeling guilty over tethering Foxy indoors. In the Dog World, such pushy behaviour would earn Foxy a good, sharp hiding from the leader, so don't worry; clipping her on a leash inside isn't cruel at all. It also isn't forever. When Foxy sees you're not going to let her take control of your important inner den in this way, she'll stop trying.

To help Foxy behave, help her relax by yawning slowly, blinking sleepily and ignoring her while you watch TV. These relaxing signals will eventually settle her down and put her in snooze mode. Now your family can watch TV in peace.

And from now on, Foxy won't be hogging the TV.

Victory lap

Mungo loves to play fetch the ball with me but I'm fast losing interest in this game. I go out with the best of intentions to play, but after a few throws, Mungo spoils the game by stupidly refusing to bring back the ball to me. Sometimes he drops the ball on the lawn halfway between us — but when I go to pick it up, he dashes in before me and bolts off with it. He then runs round and round the yard, completely ignoring me. I get so frustrated, I go inside, but he just starts barking loudly through the glass door at me and won't stop. What on earth is his problem?

Mungo's worked out you're a fantastic opponent to play ball games with — because you always lose! In the Dog

World, the winner of any ball game is the one who ends up holding the ball. By deliberately not returning the ball to you, Mungo's winning this game very quickly.

He's also really enjoying telling you that you've lost the game to him. That race around the yard with the ball in his mouth is his glorious victory lap. He's taunting you to race after him and try to wrestle it back, but you keep admitting defeat by going inside.

His barks through the glass door are him shouting at you, Hey, loser, come back out here if you dare! Try to get this ball off me again! Come on — I dare you!

He's feeling very self-important because of his easy victory, so he's got a lot of adrenaline pumping through him, and that's making his barks sharp and loud.

I think it's time you stopped handing Mungo so many easy ball victories. Firstly, you have to decide whether your dog will even play the fetch game with you.

Some dogs really don't have any desire to retrieve balls for humans — it's simply not in their breeding. If Mungo's one of those breeds, then there's no point in playing fetch with him. He only wants to grab that precious ball so he can sit down and chew it and show off that he's won final possession of it.

If Mungo's this sort of dog, pick up the ball while he's busy eating his dinner and throw it out forever. No dog should have a chance to collect ball trophies — they make dogs feel too important.

If Mungo does like playing fetch, but is deliberately trying to score points from you by not returning the ball, then you have to start getting clever.

First, I want you to throw all your old balls in the bin. Mungo's won control of these trophies too often in the past — so he'll fight very hard not to lose these particular balls in the future. Instead, buy some new balls that no-one's had a chance to win yet. Now start treating these new balls as very special, precious things.

When you next play fetch, have a couple of the new balls on hand. Throw a ball, then wait for Mungo to pick it up and turn to see your reaction. Now make a real fuss of your second ball. Throw it around in the air and keep catching it. Sound excited and happy as you play around with it. Treat it as if it's the most precious, fun thing you own.

Now step away from Mungo in a playful way, but don't look at him; instead, look lovingly at your ball and say, 'Who's got the ball? I have it! Are you coming to get it, Mungo? Come on!'

You get the idea: really tempt him into wanting your second ball. As Mungo drops the first ball at your feet so he can freely chase the second ball, you can simply reach down and pick up the ball he dropped.

Keep alternating balls in this way until you've had enough. End the game by raising your chin high and firmly saying, 'Enough!' Hold up a food reward for Mungo to see. Toss it on the ground after you pretend to nibble it. When he drops the last ball to get the treat, you can pick up the ball easily.

Now yawn slowly, blink sleepily, raise your chin and walk away. This will calm Mungo down from the exciting game and get him out of his competitive mood.

To be the winner of this game, you have to make sure you always win final possession of both balls. Keep them in a drawer when you finish playing so Mungo can't sneak off with them later.

Aah ... a clever victory tastes so sweet, doesn't it?

The trophy cabinet

Why does my dog Norman leave all his toys around his bed and out in the middle of the backyard? And why does he grab the toys back off me if I ever pick them up?

After Norman wins a toy from anyone in your family he needs to show everyone how dominant he is, so he leaves the toys he's won around his bed and in the middle of your backyard. These are his collection of prized victory trophies and he needs to show them off in a very prominent place. You could say his bed is also his trophy cabinet.

Sometimes Norman may celebrate an important win by trotting around the yard with the toy in his mouth and his tail cheekily up like a banner. This is his victory lap as he shows off his newly won trophy.

But toys aren't fun things in the Dog World. All dogs take them very seriously — especially as they mature. Norman believes his precious trophy collection is worth guarding. Trophies help show everyone why he should be the leader. They prove how fit, clever and persistent he is — all the qualities needed in a good dog leader.

The trouble is, one day Norman might nip someone if they try to take one of his hard-won trophies. Visitors and children are particularly vulnerable to these types of nips. In fact, some of the worst dog attacks happen when a visiting child accidently picks up one of these valuable dog trophies and is savaged. It's a particularly scary idea because children always want to pick up brightly coloured or furry commercial dog toys. These eye-catching, fun objects are kid-magnets; they look exactly like children's toys. If I had my way, all dog toys would be banned. This is because dogs never just 'play' with toys. Dogs only use toys to dominate. So why buy your dog something he's deliberately going to use to dominate you?

Commercial dog toys aren't the only kind of trophies dogs try to use against humans. Dogs can turn almost anything into a victory trophy: balls, socks, shoes, sticks, old bits of clothing — you get the idea. I believe commercial dog toys usually become very powerful trophies for dogs because their owners treat them as more important than old socks and sticks. The more attention a toy gets from a human, the more powerful it becomes in your dog's eyes.

However, the most dangerous dog trophies of all are your children's real toys. Dogs love stealing toys off children and turning them into victory trophies. So always keep an eye on your children's toys and make sure Norman knows he's never allowed to touch them. You don't want your kids getting nipped for picking up one of their own toys from Norman's bed.

My attitude to dog trophies is simple: get rid of your dog's entire trophy collection straightaway. The easiest way to do this is to clip Norman on a leash and attach it to something secure, then find every dog trophy lying around your house and backyard and throw them out! Yes — even his favourites have to go!

One of my favourite mottos is 'No dog should have a trophy cabinet — they just make dogs feel too ambitious'. In the future, every time you spot a dog trophy, bin it!

Welcome to Dog Land

My dog Rufus is gorgeous: exuberant and happy, but I have to admit he does wear me down with all his running around. He races around the verandahs and constantly dashes through the house. He also gets carried away and digs up my beautiful garden, especially when I give him bones. I hate nagging him to calm down all the time but I can't let him destroy my house and garden. What do you suggest I do?

I believe every dog should have a special place where they feel free to be an energetic, playful dog. The best way to do this is to have a decent-sized pen in your backyard that Rufus can't escape from. I call this pen Dog Land.

Dog Land must have some shade, shelter and plenty of drinking water. Make it as large as you can afford, and enclose it with sturdy wire mesh. Ensure your dog can't dig his way out under the fence. In Dog Land, Rufus can have raw bones to chew, run around as much as he likes and dig it up to his heart's content. The only thing he mustn't do in here is bark; like the rest of your territory, make sure Dog Land stays a bark-free zone. If you wish, you can disguise the pen by clever landscaping, but ideally Rufus should be able to see you.

Put Rufus in Dog Land as soon as you see him running around full of energy, or starting to dig up the garden. You might like to keep him in his pen whenever you leave him at home alone, such as when you go to work. You may also find it's a great place to put him when visitors come over.

However, I don't believe Dog Land should be a prison. Dogs are social creatures and need to spend time with us around the house. In particular, Rufus needs to spend time every evening with you. This could be indoors, perhaps in your living room while you watch TV, or on your verandah if you can be out there with him. If Rufus is a bother around the house, simply secure him on a leash and give him a mat to lie on.

However, for those times when you can't supervise Rufus, Dog Land is the perfect place to put him.

Help! My dog hates Dog Land

I followed your advice and built a dog pen for my dog Bess but she keeps barking to be let out. I think she hates it in there. I'd like to find a way to get her to accept the pen because she wrecks my garden when I'm at work. Please help!

When Bess barks in this way, she's telling you, I DEMAND you let me out of here! How DARE you try to keep a very important leader like ME in some sort of cage. As the leader I get to go where I like, when I like — so hurry up and let me out of here RIGHT NOW!

The next time you put Bess in her pen, make sure you've exhausted her beforehand with a good, tiring walk. Tired dogs are quiet dogs. When you put her in the pen after her walk, throw in a raw bone to keep her distracted while you shut the gate on her and go away. If she's had enough exercise, all she should want to do is lie down and chew her delicious bone in peace.

Don't make the mistake of continuing to stand there, watching her and talking to her through the wire mesh, or she'll think you're asking her to bark at you. Instead, calmly lift your chin and walk away in an aloof manner as you yawn sleepily.

If she starts to bark in protest, march back to the pen immediately, growl at her in warning and say curtly, 'Enough!' In other words, you're telling her, I'm your boss and I demand you stop that demanding barking RIGHT NOW! The moment she stops barking, lift your chin even higher and walk back inside the house. Repeat if you have to. She's just testing to see if you're going to weaken and let her out.

If she's being particularly stubborn and won't stop barking — but she doesn't show aggression towards you — then march straight into her pen, close the gate behind you, and barge through her with your chin raised. Glare at her as you growl, and again tell her, 'Enough!'

You're not barging to hurt her. You're barging through her so she'll step quickly back out of your way. With every step you get her to move backwards out of your personal space, you're earning the right to tell her to shut up.

Persevere until she's not barking at all — not even soft little barks in the back of her throat. Quite simply, this solution comes down to a matter of willpower: who's more determined to win this challenge, you or Bess?

Stop barging Bess the moment she stops barking. Walk away, still ignoring her.

It may take Bess a few weeks to completely accept the pen if she's an extremely dominant dog, but most dogs give in quickly. Like I said earlier, make sure she's exhausted by a walk and give her a raw bone to distract her. Exhausted dogs don't have much energy left over for bossy barking; all they want to do is chew a bone, snooze and relax.

Hey! I know a great way to tire myself out ... I'm going to bark nonstop!

My dog Spud races around and around our backyard, barking his head off. He's a herding breed, but all that barking is pretty annoying. How can I stop it?

Spud's desperately trying to tell you he's not getting enough exercise. It takes a lot of energy to bark — so he's trying to use up all his energy any way he can — by barking loudly as he races around. This sort of barking is a sign of extreme stress and you should do something about it immediately.

The solution is simple, but will take a lot of willpower on your part. Start taking Spud for at least one good walk — but preferably two walks — a day. Give him a nice raw bone to chew when he returns from each walk, as chewing also uses up a lot of energy. Ideally, find a place where you can take Spud swimming every day as this really exhausts energetic dogs.

Once Spud's getting enough exercise without fail every single day, then you've earned the right to make your property a Bark-free Zone. Insist that Spud never barks on your property again. If he barks after you give the command

'Enough!', raise your chin and barge through him until he stops.

If you're a natural couch potato, I don't believe you should own an energetic herding dog like Spud, but if you do then it's up to you to give him the exercise he needs to be happy. Just think how healthy you're going to be doing a fine walk every day. Spud's going to be your new personal trainer!

How do you stop a dog roaming?

I'm at my wit's end because our dog Polly has begun to roam. She's desexed and gets really good walks every few days. I've never had this problem before as our last dog Fred never roamed off our property at all.

There's only one way to guarantee a dog doesn't roam and that's to invest in an escape-proof yard or a decent-sized pen.

If you can't afford this just yet, put up a good dog run. This is a cheaper alternative to a pen. It's usually a sturdy peg with a long chain or cable leash connected, so your dog can still race around. Some dog runs have the cable stretched between two pegs, or stakes, with a leash that clips to the cable. This allows the dog to race up and down the length of the cable. You can buy kit versions of runs, or make your own. Make sure there's shelter, shade and plenty of fresh water. Hide some raw bones around.

It's also essential you walk Polly every day, as no backyard or pen is ever big enough — or exciting enough — to replace walks off the property. I know you may not want to hear this, but I believe dogs are happier with two routine walks a day, rather than a long walk every few days. Since dogs are natural predators, those two walks are the highlights of their day because they resemble going out for an exciting morning and afternoon hunt.

However, don't make the mistake of leaving Polly permanently in her pen or on her run. Every afternoon and evening, bring your dog inside your house or at least up onto your verandah. All dogs need to spend quality time with you around the house.

To stop Polly escaping from your house, tether her on a leash when she comes inside, or when she's on the verandah. Otherwise she may push past someone using the door and escape out onto the street.

I know some people claim their dog never leaves their property, but they're usually unaware that their dog has disappeared for a while. Almost all dogs who have freedom will roam at least as far as the area just outside your property — if only to scent-mark. Some dogs will scent-mark their way around the immediate neighbourhood before returning home.

Don't risk Polly getting accidently run over, attacked by another dog, causing an incident, or getting picked up by the dog ranger. Put her in a pen or fence your yard securely. It's the only way to stop Polly roaming.

Banished to Outer Siberia

My husband got sick of our dog Victor causing mess and destruction around our house, so he put him in a dog run with a kennel down in the bottom corner of the backyard. Although he has plenty of grassy space to run around in, Victor constantly barks and howls down there. I can't give him the freedom of our house — he just destroys it! What do you suggest I do?

Victor's feeling miserable because spending all his time so far away from your den and the rest of your family is making him isolated and lonely. Dogs are such sociable creatures, they really need to feel they belong. To Victor, it's as if you've banished him permanently to Outer Siberia.

When Victor barks and howls miserably, he's saying, BARK! BARK! What have I done to be sent all the way out here? I want to be in the den with the rest of you. Please let me be part of the pack again. BARK! BARK! Let me spend time with you, please … pleeeease … hooooooooowl … hoooooooowl … hoooooooowl.

To be a truly happy dog, Victor has to spend quality time with you and your family on your verandah or inside your house. This means you should bring him up to the house at least each evening. I believe all dogs need to spend quality time relaxing with their family of an evening. This is the time when dog packs laze around the inner den together, really chilling out and bonding.

If you can't trust Victor to be free inside your house, tether him on a mat in your living room while the family watches TV, or to a railing on the verandah if that's where your family will be. Once he's tethered on a leash, you'll be surprised at how quickly Victor learns respectful house manners. Try to bring him up to the house several times during the day as well.

Ideally, Victor should also be able to sleep near your family every night. Start by bringing his bedding up to the house. For example, you could put his dog bed inside your laundry or on the verandah, if there's shelter. If you tether his leash to something fixed, such as a railing or a sturdy wall hook, Victor won't be able to move much further than his bed — and he won't be able to cause mess and havoc. In the morning put Victor back on his dog run for a run around, and give him a raw bone to chew to keep him distracted.

You can't expect Victor to feel he's a vital part of your pack if he can't see the family or the house properly, so consider moving his dog run closer to the house. If you feel he might destroy your garden, consider building a dog pen instead and landscape around it to hide the mesh.

However, even if you move his run closer, Victor still needs to come up to the house. Dogs love spending time with their humans. Don't let Victor lead an isolated existence, banished permanently to the bottom of your backyard. It's time to invite poor, lonely Victor in from Outer Siberia!

The ambush monster

My little dog Minnie is a bit of a monster. If someone walks past on the footpath outside our house, she loves to ambush them by running out and nipping them on the back of the ankle. Why is she acting like an aggressive guard dog when she's so little? I don't mind her having her freedom out the front of our house — we live in a quiet cul-de-sac — but I want to stop these embarrassing ambushes. Some regular walkers on our road are getting quite nasty about it. Have you any suggestions?

The trouble here is that Minnie's stretched her territory beyond your property to include the public footpath as well. Every morning when she's been going outside your front garden to do a wee, she's actually been scent-marking an extra piece of real estate to add to her territory.

It's a bit like a dot-to-dot puzzle: if you joined up all Minnie's scent-marks you'd find an invisible fence. This kind of wee-fence is very obvious to other dogs, but we humans are totally unaware of them.

As a human walks past your house on this footpath, Minnie thinks, HEY YOU, INTRUDER, you're invading my territory! I know you can smell my wee-fence warning because I just freshened it up a little while ago. How DARE you ignore it and saunter onto my personal territory. Well, now I'm going to chase you off … YAP! YAP! YAP! YAP! *Nip!*

Even little dogs hurt when they nip, so Minnie's empire-building has to end today — before she lands herself — and you — in serious legal trouble.

The only way to stop her from guarding the footpath outside your home is to keep her in a secure yard with no view of the street. You can't allow her the freedom to wander off your property again. Don't even allow her to scent-mark around the gate when you take her for a walk on the leash.

There's no other reliable way of stopping dogs from guarding their territories; the natural guarding instinct is just too strong in some dogs — especially little empire-builders like Minnie.

Remember, in the Dog World, if she can wee on it, then she's earned the right to aggressively protect it.

Fence line fury

I'm at my wits' end: my dog Dexter won't stop barking at my neighbour's dog, Mimi. We live in suburbia with a paling fence between our two properties and our two dogs race up and down the fence line, barking their heads off at each other. I'm constantly shouting at Dexter to shut up, but he usually ignores me. I don't think Dexter and Mimi want to fight, but between them they certainly make a lot of noise.

When Dexter barks at Mimi through the fence, he's telling her, Hey, Mimi! I challenge you to run up and down this fence! Let's see who can keep it up the longest and do it with the most noise! Are you up for the challenge?

The winner is the dog who can outrun, out-bark and outlast the other dog. Bored, under-exercised dogs in suburbia really love this challenge, so it's definitely time to channel all that energy into something quieter.

For a start, you have to immediately increase Dexter's exercise. In my opinion, if a dog isn't lying around quietly during the day, then he isn't getting enough exercise. On the return from the walk, give Dexter a raw bone to chew. Chewing bones takes a lot of energy and strength and helps tire a dog out wonderfully. Dogs also find chewing bones relaxing.

You could also discuss with your neighbour the need for Mimi to have more exercise, too. Explain that a tired dog is a well-behaved dog. The hardest thing involving two barking dogs is getting both neighbours to agree on solving the problem at the same time.

Now let's discuss your fence line. If Dexter and Mimi can

see each other from only a few centimetres away through the palings, neither dog will be able to stop challenging the other to this noisy contest.

Solve this by erecting a sturdy wire-mesh fence to prevent Dexter reaching the paling fence, and densely plant it with shrubs. Now you have extra space dividing the two dogs and blocking their sight of each other.

How do you stop the barking in the meantime? Teach Dexter your property is now a Bark-free Zone. No dog has the right to run around making unnecessary noise, and as no lead dog would accept it, neither should you.

Set aside a weekend to really break this insolent barking habit. Secure Dexter on a leash up near the house or on the verandah where you can easily get to him. As soon as he barks, march out there with your chin raised. Look down at him from the corner of your eye and growl in warning, then say, 'Enough!'

If he ignores you, raise your chin and barge straight through him until he stops. March inside again. Do this as often as you need to until he decides barking at Mimi simply isn't worth it. Of course, you'll make your job so much easier if you exhaust Dexter with plenty of exercise and give him some raw bones to chew.

Be firm. Dexter has to learn the new rule: no more barking at Mimi through the fence!

Dexter does it again

I've done what you suggested but Dexter still barks back at Mimi through the fence. What can I do now?

Stopping Dexter from barking back at Mimi after you've let him get away with it for so long is going to be hard but you have to persevere and win — or you'll be listening to his annoying barking forever.

Be prepared to constantly tell Dexter to be quiet the first weekend you introduce your Bark-free Zone. However, most dogs will keep testing you every now and again for at least another three weeks — if not longer. This sort of barking has become a habit for Dexter, so it will take more than a few days to break it.

Continue to secure Dexter on the leash near the house where you can get to him quickly. It will help if you make Dexter realise how serious an offence any barking is now, so look and sound very angry when you walk outside to barge through him to make him be quiet. After all, you're the leader and this disrespectful follower is constantly making you waste your precious energy by walking outside to reprimand him.

Until he learns to be quiet, I want you to be much more aloof with him. I also want you to stop giving him any pats and attention; don't even look at him. A dog that's being deliberately ignored by the leader will naturally start feeling more submissive and quiet.

As exhausted as you may get, you really do have to go outside every single time Dexter barks. From now onwards there's not to be a bark, a whine or even a peep from him. Peeps quickly turn into nonstop barking if you allow them to continue.

You can also make it easier for Dexter to avoid being triggered off by Mimi if you take away his view of the troublesome fence line. Build a dog run (see page 105 for how to do this) in an area of your yard that has no view of the fence line shared with Mimi. Keep Dexter clipped on this dog run for a few weeks — especially when you leave your property and can't supervise him. If you don't want to invest in a dog run, use a length of chain, or buy plastic-coated dog-run wire from a pet shop. If you don't like the idea of a dog run, then build Dexter a dog pen instead. Now you'll have a place with no view of the fence to leave him when you're not at home.

Once you've got this barking problem licked, you can release Dexter again. If he starts the barking again, all you have to do is clip him back on his dog run.

Barking problems can be exhausting to break, but it's definitely possible. It's just a matter of making sure your willpower is much stronger than Dexter's.

Good luck!

Visitor invasion

Why does my dog Dumbo always run out and greet my friends by racing around, barking his head off and behaving like a stupid maniac? Please help me stop his really annoying behaviour.

Dumbo isn't as stupid as you think. There's a good reason why he's acting like a maniac around your visitors: he regards them as intruders invading his territory and he's trying to grab control of them by winning plenty of challenges.

He achieves this by ensuring he's the first to meet your visitors the moment they walk inside the gate. He can lure them into submissively patting him. He can invade the visitors' personal space by dominantly jumping up on them. He can bark noisily so no-one else can be heard. He can race around, herding everyone together. He can deliberately trip people over. He can step on their feet. He can force people to take submissive detours around him. And, finally, he can race through the front door first to show he owns the inside of your house as well. The result? If Dumbo wins that many victories then he easily wins the right to be the boss of everyone.

It's simple to stop your dog annoying your visitors. When you know visitors are about to arrive, clip Dumbo on a secured leash out in your backyard. When your friends arrive, ask them to completely ignore him for the entire visit. Dumbo should soon switch off and relax.

After an hour or so of him being submissively quiet, you can try unclipping him, but ask your friends to continue ignoring him. If he starts misbehaving, all you have to do is clip him back on his leash.

Barking on the leash

As you suggested, I tied up Dumbo before the visitors arrived, but now he won't stop barking. What do I do next?

Dumbo is demanding, How dare you put me on this leash! I am your boss: release me at once so I can go over and dominate those pesky intruders!

Luckily, there's a way you can stop him. Every time Dumbo barks, raise your chin, fold your arms and march angrily over to where he's clipped on his leash. Then barge straight through him until he stops barking and gets subserviently out of your way.

As you barge through him, glare down at him from the corner of your eye, growl at him, then say curtly, 'Enough!'

The moment Dumbo stops barking, walk away. Help him relax by yawning slowly and blinking sleepily as you walk back to your friends. Do this as often as you need to until he stays quiet.

This method isn't designed to hurt Dumbo; it's about getting him to step backwards submissively out of your way. With every step you make him take backwards, you're earning the right to tell him to shut up.

As for your friends, if they tense up and turn around to watch, Dumbo will bark even more. The best thing they can do is to turn away and keep chatting. They should ignore him no matter what he does.

Once Dumbo lies down quietly, leave him for an hour or so to settle before you try unclipping him again. He will stop testing you once he realises you're completely serious about your new rule: no more barking around visitors!

Call of duty

My dog Murphy hates people in uniform. He seems to think they're a major threat when really they're just people going about their job — like the postie and electricity-meter reader. When uniformed people step onto my property, Murphy runs out at them barking aggressively. I'm scared that one day he's going to bite someone. Is there a way I can train this guarding instinct out of him?

I think Murphy doesn't like humans in uniform because they act in such a purposeful way around our territory. For example, Murphy might look at the electricity-meter reader and think, Why's that human walking with such intent onto our territory? Is he trying to grab control of our territory? Well, I'm not sure what his purpose is but, whatever it is, I don't like it. So BARK! BARK! BARK! I'M WARNING YOU — GET OFF MY TERRITORY RIGHT NOW!

However, what Murphy thinks is irrelevant. He can't keep guarding your territory against people in uniform or he's going to land himself in deep trouble. I believe the only solution to this problem is to keep a natural guard dog like Murphy in a secure pen or on a very secure dog run when he's not under your direct supervision.

You will never truly take that kind of natural guarding instinct out of Murphy because it's been carefully bred into him for too many generations. If he does end up listening to his instincts and biting someone, then he'll probably pay for his mistake with his life. You'll also have to pay some very hefty legal bills.

It's time to stop taking risks. If you're determined that Murphy should run freely around your property, then you must erect a secure, high, escape-proof fence around your house. Install a locked, secure gate with an intercom service, so that people can enter only after you buzz them in. Contact all your meter readers and make suitable arrangements. Signpost your property with warning notices and provide a cell-phone number so you are always contactable.

I want you to start taking all aggression in dogs very seriously. It's your responsibility to make sure Murphy doesn't hurt anyone. I've asked some meter readers to show me their scars and they were horrendous. These people are just trying to do their job — they shouldn't have to risk their lives.

Whenever I get high ...

Mack, our dog, loves rushing up the stairs ahead of me and then looking down as I walk up towards him. In fact, he adores getting higher than me any chance he can. For example, he also loves running up to the balcony and looking down at me in the garden. Why is this, do you think?

One challenge dogs really love winning is getting higher than you. It naturally makes them feel dominant and can quickly put them in a misbehaving sort of mood.

In future, get Mack to walk behind you up any stairs. If he ignores your firm command, 'Back!', nudge him back with your knee if he tries to run ahead of you. Stay firm but calm. Don't watch him. Instead, raise your chin high and bump him back with your knee as he tries to rush up past you.

If Mack still keeps barging past you, leave a leash ready nearby so you can make him re-walk the stairs, only this time with him submissively behind you. When he learns you're not going to let him get away with it, he'll stop trying to push past you rudely.

When you're in the garden, foil Mack's dominant balcony act by simply ignoring him. Pretend he doesn't exist. Raise your chin very high and look away. Ignoring another dog is an extremely dominant thing to do in the Dog World and helps to neutralise Mack's challenge. The worst thing you can do is stare up at him, as this will make him feel he's winning.

So now you know: the higher your dog gets above you — the more he thinks he's dominating you.

Balcony barker

My dog Dollar loves to sit out on our front balcony and enjoy a high view over our road. This was okay when he was young, but now it's become a real problem. He barks at absolutely everything that passes by: people, dogs, bikes, cars; you name it, he'll bark at it. Now the neighbours are starting to complain about the noise. What can I do?

Dollar believes that when you allow him up on the balcony, you're actually putting him on guard duty as a look-out scout! He's only doing what comes naturally for all dogs — using a high place with a view to warn off potential intruders.

So let's take Dollar off duty. From now on, make that balcony off-limits to Dollar. You may need to erect a toddler barricade that prevents him getting out onto the balcony. You can buy these from baby-equipment stores.

If Dollar continues to bark from your front yard, or from windows inside your house that face the street, move him out to your backyard so he can't see the road at all. Block his view of the road by using solid fencing or shrubs if you need to.

Remember, if you allow your dog out the front of your house, you're asking him to go on guard duty. Being kept out the back means he's off-duty. Don't let your dog bark out the back.

If you want your dog to stop barking up on the balcony, take away his high view of the front road. Dollar, it's time you got an honourable discharge from guard duty!

Night barking for no reason

My dog Mufti must be paranoid. At night when he sleeps in his kennel outside, he keeps barking at nothing at all. When I yell at him out the window to shut up, he goes quiet for a while, then starts up the minute I sit down again. I've tried whacking him, but that only made me feel bad, and it didn't work anyway. I don't want to get rid of him, but my neighbour's complaints are getting even more annoying than Mufti's barking. What can I do?

Whatever the reason for Mufti's barking, he can't keep it up — or you're going to get a hefty fine.

This is one way you can stop him. When Mufti next barks at night, calmly walk outside and clip him on a leash to his kennel.

With your chin raised, growl down at him from the corner of your eye — then walk back inside. You just told him, As the leader, I came out because you barked in warning. I checked for danger and there was none. You've just wasted my precious energy by calling me all the way out here for nothing. I'm warning you, don't waste my time like that again.

The next time Mufti barks, march back out to him in a very aggressive, no-nonsense manner and barge straight through him with your arms folded and your chin raised high so he stops barking. Give a deep, warning growl as you glare down at him from the corner of your eye, and say, 'Enough!'

Do this as many times as you need to, until Mufti decides it isn't worth barking at nothing. The majority of dogs will give in after a few nights of testing you out — although very dominant dogs can test you for weeks.

The idea is to have zero tolerance to any sort of barking at all from now on. Even a small bark should get you erupting straight out there and marching through him until he stops and steps backwards. The more steps backwards he takes, the more submissive he'll feel. Be inexhaustible and very sure of yourself.

Don't weaken and show your dog any affection. Don't let him bark for a while in the hope he'll eventually give up. You have to stop him barking every single time as soon as you can. It will really help if you exhaust him every day with two good walks. A tired dog is a quiet dog. A nicely exhausted dog is a totally silent dog!

This is a simple solution, but you need to be determined that you're going to stop Mufti night barking forever.

If you really can't barge through your dog or growl in a way he'll believe, consider moving Mufti inside your laundry at night and tethering him on a leash so he can't get far from his bed. Once he's inside, Mufti will probably stop barking as much because he'll feel more secure, being in the 'inner den' with the rest of the pack. However, you'll still have to come to him every time he barks and sternly say, 'Enough!'

Pure perseverance will win this battle of wills. If you truly want success, never surrender! Don't let Mufti's barking beat you.

Don't touch my mobile territory!

Why does Bobby, our little dog, protect our car so aggressively? He's really friendly around our house and welcomes guests with a wagging tail. But when it comes to the car Bobby transforms into a terrible little 'car wolf'! He psychotically defends the car — even from people innocently walking past — and this is while I'm in the car with him. (I never leave him alone in the car.) What do you suggest I do about this embarrassing car-guarding aggression?

Bobby obviously thinks he's earned the right to be in charge of your car. In his eyes, your car is a little mobile piece of your territory — and he's definitely the boss of it.

How did Bobby take charge of your car? Think about his behaviour on the way to your destination. Did he stand up dominantly high and stare out the window — or perhaps (even more dominantly) stick his head right out the window? Height with a view always makes little dogs feel far too important. Did Bobby bark out the window as you drove? That would have made him feel extremely important. Did he get to race around the inside of the car doing whatever he wanted? This kind of chaotic freedom will also help inflate his ego. Did you let him sit on your lap? He'll feel very dominant invading your personal space like that.

By the time you park the car at your destination, little Bobby definitely feels as if he's earned the right to be your leader — and the boss of the car. As the leader, one of his jobs is to guard the car from intruders. And if you've let him scent-mark on your tyres, then he's not going to want anyone stepping near your car at all. Some little dogs also get a real high from barking and scaring off humans from their car — especially all the small ratting breeds, who've had plenty of courage and noisy, intimidating barks bred into them.

As Bobby barks at passers-by, he's telling them, Beware, this car is mine! I earned the right to be in charge of guarding it on the trip over here. This is part of our mobile territory, and I was born to guard it — so that's what I'm going to do, no matter how big and scary you are. YAP! YAP! YAP! Ha ha, watch that human walking away quickly — I just successfully chased her away!

So how can we retire Bobby from his mobile security-guard job? Until he stops behaving in such a disrespectful way in the car, start tethering him on a short leash on the back seat. Now he can't win control of the car on the trip over by racing around. If he won't stop barking, secure him so he's down on the floor and doesn't have a view out the window. Of course, every state has its own laws regarding dogs travelling in cars, so check with the relevant authority in your state to ensure your dog is lawfully restrained.

While you're parked, keep Bobby clipped on his leash in the back seat (and never leave him alone in the car). Don't let him sit on your lap; this is such a dominant place for little dogs to sit — and it's exactly why they like sitting there.

If Bobby barks or growls at anyone going past, raise your chin and glare at him in warning out of the corner of your eye, as you say firmly, 'Leave it!'

Sorry, Bobby, your days as an over-protective car wolf are over, so just sit back and enjoy the trip.

3

Kids and Dogs

Kids and dogs are a wonderful sight together, but if you don't supervise them it can lead to trouble, such as barging, nips or worse. If you follow a few simple rules, however, kids and dogs can co-exist happily. In this section I explain why your child should always be treated more importantly than your dog — and I'll also show you how to recognise when your dog's asking you for help.

My dog adores it when my daughter hugs him!

I don't believe you when you say dogs hate being hugged. I know Lewis, our big dog, absolutely loves it when my daughter Selena lies on him and hugs him. He lies down like a gentle giant and closes his eyes in bliss. He even smiles as he pants and occasionally wags his tail. Why are you so against hugging?

I'm not against hugging, but I want humans to hug other humans, not dogs. As I explained in 'Dog Language' (see pages 9–89), dogs view hugs as fight-holds. For this reason, children should never be allowed to hug dogs.

Lewis thinks that your daughter is openly challenging him to a play-fight when she hugs him. In fact, in his view Selena's being especially challenging because she's lying dominantly all over him while she does it.

Lewis, bless his gentle heart, is obviously a very respectful gentleman of a dog. He's doing everything he can not to hurt your daughter. Even though he doesn't like being hugged, he has politely slumped down and is playing dead, hoping your young human pup will eventually get bored and stop playing her mock-fighting game with him.

You can tell Lewis is stressed by his bursts of stressed panting and that confused, heavy tail wag that thumps the ground every now and again. And when he licks her face or hand, he's politely and submissively begging her to stop challenging him.

As you can imagine, not all dogs are going to be as polite as Lewis. Hugging dogs is how many children end up getting nipped — whether by the family dog or by a dog they don't know.

So please teach your daughter that no dog likes being hugged, including poor, stressed-out Lewis.

New baby

My husband, Tom, and I are expecting our first baby in three weeks, and I'm concerned about how our four-year-old dog, Robbie, will react. He seems very aloof with the children he meets. I have to admit, we've always treated Robbie as our little baby and now I'm worried he's going to be jealous. Do you have any suggestions?

You have every reason to be concerned. If Robbie's been treated like a human child all his life, then he's obviously been allowed to win many challenges over the years from you and Tom. By now, no doubt he considers himself to be the undisputed leader of you both. If you continue to treat him in the same way, then he'll also believe he's the boss of your baby. This gives him the right to nip your baby if he feels the child's being treated as more important than him. You have three weeks to change his attitude. Use the time to make Robbie feel as unimportant as possible. From now on, Robbie has to feel that he's the least important member of your family.

Start by taking away Robbie's freedom. Now he won't feel like the king of the castle. Start tethering Robbie on a leash when he comes inside and give him his own mat to sit on. Place this mat in a corner of the main family room and make sure it's out of everyone's way — perhaps in a corner. It's almost impossible for a dog to remain the leader when he isn't allowed any freedom to roam around the house winning endless challenges from everyone.

If you have a yard, build Robbie a pen so he can get used to spending time outside in it. Introduce Robbie to the pen after he's had a good, energetic walk so he's too tired to bark much in protest. When he's put in the pen, help him settle down by giving him a raw bone or two. This will help persuade him the pen can be a good, relaxing place to be.

Now you've organised for Robbie to have places both inside and outside where you can secure him whenever you're busy with your baby. You're also sending him a clear message, You're no longer the leader around here because you no longer have too much freedom.

From now on, I also want you and Tom to stop giving Robbie so much affection and attention. For example, stop watching him so much. Instead, raise your chin and act in a much more aloof way when you're around him. Relax him by turning your head away, yawning slowly and blinking sleepily. This body language sends him a clear, strong message, Don't panic just because I'm starting to act like an aloof leader. I'm good at taking charge now, so relax.

During the next three weeks keep using your body language to emphasise to Robbie how dominant you are. The more aloofly you behave, the more Robbie will see you as his leader. But never forget to act like a relaxed aloof leader.

Too many affectionate pats will start making Robbie feel important again, so instead of patting Robbie, a better way to show affection is to ask Tom to walk him more often, but make sure he stays on the leash to keep him in a submissive frame of mind.

Finally, never leave your baby alone with or in reach of Robbie because, put simply, the baby should never be Robbie's concern. I sincerely urge you never to take risks with your baby's safety. Babies are completely defenceless.

Introducing the baby to Robbie

How should we introduce the new baby to Robbie? I've heard so many different ideas about how to do this. What do you suggest?

Personally, I don't believe Robbie should have much to do with your baby at all. Mother dogs don't encourage other dogs to go near their newborn pups, so this should be your safe attitude too.

For example, once you bring your baby home, don't walk over and offer Robbie a look or smell of your newborn, as this will make him feel far too important. Think about it: if you take your baby to him, you're taking Submissive Steps towards him and making him the centre of attention. You're asking him, Do you accept my pup, Boss?

Instead, when you come home from the hospital, give Robbie minimum attention. This will remind him yet again that he's the least important member of your family. It's crucial that Robbie always regards your baby as being much more important than him.

Ask your husband, Tom, to keep him exhausted with plenty of exercise and walks. A tired dog won't have much energy left over for challenging anyone, including your baby.

I think it's a great idea if you take the baby with you for some of these walks because sharing a walk is a great way for a pack to bond without having to touch each other. Just walking along together will be enough of an introduction between Robbie and your baby.

Over the next few months, Robbie will get to know your baby simply because he'll see your child in your arms. He'll sniff from a distance. He'll come on lots of family walks with you. However, I'd never allow your dog inside your baby's safe bubble of personal space. As a follower, he has no right — or need — to get so close to your baby.

Remember: nonstop licking, nudging for pats and standing still above your baby are not signs of affection, they are dominating challenges. Even if Robbie really seems to accept the baby, never leave him alone with or within reach of your precious child.

When you bring Robbie inside, always keep him tethered on his leash mat. Now he still feels like part of the family, but he won't get any opportunities to sneak over and try to dominate your baby while your back is turned.

You can help take away Robbie's desire to challenge your baby if you act in a very relaxed, confident way. Every now and then look away from Robbie, raise your chin and yawn very slowly and blink really sleepily. Now you're letting him know, Relax, Robbie, I'm in control so you don't need to worry about anything — including this new baby.

If Robbie starts lying down on his mat, out of everyone's way, with his bottom to you, his chin on the floor and giving a deep sigh — then great! He's relaxed enough to ignore your child. When he behaves like this, Robbie's showing you beautiful, respectful dog manners — but never make the mistake of completely trusting him around your baby.

Heidi begs for help

Sometimes our dog Heidi comes over to me when the kids are playing with her. She stands in front of me and gazes up into my eyes with her tail low. Why is she doing this?

Heidi is desperately begging you to stop your kids from annoying her. Her low tail shows she's being submissive. Her way of gazing up into your eyes is a question. She's asking you, Boss, can you do something to sort out your boisterous pups? They won't stop annoying me and they're ignoring all my polite signals to leave me alone. Can you help me?

I hope you now realise that Heidi is showing you beautiful manners. Reward her polite behaviour immediately by telling your kids to leave Heidi alone. If you can't trust them to stop pestering her, place Heidi in a different area of the house or in a different yard. Now she'll know it's definitely worth coming to you whenever she has a problem.

Please learn to spot those wonderful moments when Heidi asks you for help.

When pushiness is disguised as friendliness

We have a beautiful, friendly dog called Anna that everyone loves. Her tail never stops wagging, she never stops smiling, she licks you on the face in greeting — but she always seems a little clumsy around our grandkids. Someone always seems to be getting bumped over, but she's always gentle and not rushing around. Is she just a bit clumsy?

Not all dogs win challenges by being rough or aggressive. Some, like Anna, can be gently pushy in the friendliest possible way.

Anna will look at your grandkids and think, I can't let these unruly human pups win control of me ... they're too rough ... they'll pull my ears, grab me around the neck in mock fight-holds, hurt my poor back by leaning on me, and jump on my paws. So how can I make myself the boss of them without being aggressive? I'll just make sure I win all the challenges very gently and in the friendliest way possible.

This is why she gently ploughs through your grandkids, wagging her tail, slowly bumping kids out of her way, casually stepping on toes, and dominantly licking their faces so they step back and give her room.

The result? She wins plenty of challenges so she can be the boss of all the grandkids — but she does it in the sweetest, friendliest and gentlest way imaginable.

Is she being a bad dog? No. It's very difficult for any dog to be submissive to kids. Why? Kids can really hurt and annoy dogs. To survive, polite dogs like Anna work out they simply act in a very friendly and gentle manner as they win all those powerful challenges, especially those that win control of personal space. Can you really blame her? I see Anna's friendly yet pushy behaviour as a necessary survival tactic.

I believe kids should always be seen as more important than dogs — but I also think dogs need to be protected from kids. So always keep an eye on Anna when she's with your grandkids to make sure they don't start being too rowdy and rough around with her. Teach the kids to respect her personal space. The kindest thing they can do is to just leave her alone so Anna can completely relax.

Just because she looks friendly, it doesn't mean she isn't stressed. Heavy panting, gazing at you, and her tail wagging low and slow are all signs that she's very stressed by all the attention and she's asking for your help.

Anna's clearly a natural-born lady. Please help protect her from your grandkids.

Oh no! The grand-monsters have arrived!

I'm a bit concerned about my mum and dad's dog, Nanna. She's getting on in years now. She's always been great with kids but lately she's been making me feel a little nervous when I bring my three children over to see their grandparents. She's growled a few times at my children and even snapped the air near them once. Why is she suddenly getting so cranky with my kids? Is she jealous?

Quite simply, Nanna is getting too old to cope with human children now. It can be very frightening for an old dog to be around energetic, unpredictable, fast-moving children. Kids being friendly can mean something completely different to an old dog. Even the friendliest, gentlest child can seem dangerously unsafe to Nanna.

Nanna knows your kids could really hurt her by leaning on her, barging her over or accidently poking her in the eye. She also hasn't got the energy to try to work out what they're going to do next so she can protect herself.

I think old dogs deserve to retire with dignity, so when you bring your family over to see your parents, ask your kids to completely ignore Nanna and pretend she isn't there. Nanna will find being ignored much more relaxing.

You can also ask your kids to help make Nanna feel safe by turning their heads away from her and slowly yawning as they arrive and leave. This tells her, We're going to leave you alone, so relax, you're safe from us.

However, if your kids can't be trusted to leave Nanna completely alone, put the old dog in a place where your kids can't reach her, say in a locked laundry or in a fenced side garden.

Now, instead of Nanna thinking, Oh no, the grand-monsters have arrived, she'll just think, Great! Some peace and quiet on my own.

Playing — or dominating?

My dog Queenie loves playing with my kids, Jessica and Alan. I heard you say on the radio that kids and dogs should never be allowed to play alone together — why is this?

You glance out the window and see Queenie in the yard with your kids. But is she playing with them, or is she dominating them?

Perhaps Queenie gently takes a toy from Jessica and carries it around in her mouth. Is this her way of playing a game with your daughter? I'm afraid not. Queenie's actually proving how much more dominant she is than your child. By taking one of your child's possessions away, in her view Queenie's earned the right to take anything away from Jessica.

By the rules of the Dog World, if you win a prized possession from someone, it becomes your trophy and you're within your rights to guard it, so if Jessica picks up a toy that Queenie's taken many times from her, your dog feels she's earned the right to nip her. Many kids get bitten this way. Please never let your dog touch any of your kids' toys. I also suggest you throw out any old toys lying around — they've already been made into trophies.

Another time, you see Queenie walk up to your son Alan and start eating something out of his hand. Are they just sharing some food? Unfortunately not. There's no such thing as sharing in the Dog World. Queenie's dominantly taking food from Alan. This will make her feel dangerously more important than your son. Now she's earned the right to nip him if he does something she doesn't like. From now on, never let your dog go near your children if they're eating.

Or perhaps you see your dog bring a stick over and offer it to Alan. Your son laughingly takes it from her. Later, Queenie picks up the stick from the ground — or takes it back from Alan. She might do this many times. Now your dog's earned the right to nip Alan if he picks up the stick again. Ask your children to ignore any sticks Queenie brings them — and never pick up any sticks near your dog.

Sometimes you might see your dog licking your daughter's face nonstop. Unfortunately, this is not the friendly and affectionate behaviour it might appear. Queenie's dominating Jessica by invading her personal space. Now she's earned the right to invade your daughter's space all the time. For example, she can barge her out of the way, jump up on her, and bump her over. She'll probably do this while your daughter's running or hurrying, so it looks like an accident. Don't let your dog lick your children nonstop.

Dogs naturally want to dominate children. They do it because they can get away with it, and because they're trying to protect themselves from getting hurt by your kids — in their view, once they've established dominance over a child, they've earned the right to discipline that child in the future. Dogs are predators, so they like to always be in control.

For all these reasons, never leave dogs and children alone together, especially to play unsupervised. There's only one reason to play games in the Dog World, and that's to win dominance over your opponent. If Queenie wins all these little games against your children then she also earns the right to dominate them. Worse, she's earned the right to nip them if they do something she doesn't like.

No matter how gentle Queenie is, there may come a day when she loses her patience and disciplines your children with a quick nip or even a short attack. Dogs have such sharp teeth! They can do so much damage to a child's skin within seconds. Please don't risk this ever happening.

I can't repeat it enough: always supervise children around dogs — especially outside. And teach your kids to leave Queenie alone while they play — again, especially outside. Explain to them that Queenie has a big invisible bubble around her and they can't go inside her big bubble for any reason when they're playing outdoors. Believe me, Queenie will relax much more if she sees your kids are respecting her personal space in this way — and she'll stop challenging them so much.

Even so, never leave her alone with your children, because even the gentlest dog can nip.

Who's more important?

My wife claims I'm always treating my dog Baz as though he's more important than my young son. It's not wrong to give your dog pats, is it?

It's not wrong to pat Baz, but it becomes a serious problem if you pat your dog more than you show affection to your son. Your dog has to get the very clear message that your son is always more important than he is. Obviously your wife is picking up something here, so listen to her maternal instincts.

Does this scenario sound familiar? You call your son to you — but Baz races over and reaches you first. You automatically reach down and affectionately pat your dog, and Baz thinks, YES! I got my human to pat me before he touched his own human pup. Therefore I must be more important than his pup.

By the time your son comes over, Baz is sitting dominantly between your knees. He demands more pats from you, and you absent-mindedly give them as you talk to your son. Now Baz is thinking, Ha! He may be talking to you, kid, but look what he's doing for me: he's patting me subserviently. Even better, he's letting me sit within the circle of his precious personal space — and you, kid, are not!

Why are these things a problem? If Baz keeps winning all these little challenges against your son, then he'll believe he's much more important. He's also earning the right to nip your kid if he does something Baz doesn't like. Many children get bitten because their parents accidently treat their dog as if it's more important than the children are.

From now on, become much more aware of the message you're giving Baz about your son. Your son should always be treated as being much more important than Baz.

Are you treating your little dog as if it's more important than anyone else in your family?

I have a little fluffy dog called Tina and she's so easy to be around. I often send all my kids away when they get too rowdy and call my little Tina over to me instead. But lately I've been catching Tina growling at my children. What's going on? She's got no reason to be jealous of my kids, because I give her far more attention than them!

Tina's not jealous of your kids. When she growls at them, she's warning them that they're not treating her with enough respect. The trouble is, Tina thinks she's much more important than your children, because you keep giving her the message that she is.

I know it's tempting to lavish attention and affection on your little dog, especially when your human kids are being difficult. But be aware of what messages you're sending Tina. If you send your kids away and then immediately call Tina to you then of course she's going to believe she's now higher ranking than they are.

This becomes dangerous because now Tina believes she's got the right to growl and even nip your children if they don't act submissively enough around her.

To fix this problem, stop making Tina feel so important. For example, after you send your children away to play, wait at least ten minutes before you call your dog to you, and always get Tina to sit submissively for you before you touch her. More importantly, when your children come over to you, stop patting Tina and send her away immediately.

Now Tina won't get confused because she's getting one consistent message from you: your children are always more important than she is!

Teenage wrestle mania

My teenage son and his friends love wrestling with our teenage dog Rover, but lately he's started nipping them quite hard. How do we stop these nips? I'm sure Rover doesn't mean to hurt the boys because he still wants to keep on playing with them afterwards.

I'll bet Rover loves wrestling with your teenage son and his friends! It's so easy winning against humans when you have a mouthful of sharp teeth.

In the Dog World, playful wrestling is a game that's often used by teenage dogs to work out which is the naturally dominant leader of the group. Wrestling is a good way for young dogs to practice and perfect all their favourite fight-holds and other winning manoeuvres.

Every time Rover wins each wrestle game with a nip, he's telling your son and his friends, Yep! As usual I won that game with a nice, sharp victory nip. You stopped playing, so I'm definitely the boss of you.

This is why you should never let humans play wrestle games with dogs, no matter how much fun they seem.

Dogs take these games incredibly seriously. Rover's only a teenager and, as he gets older, he's going to turn those nips into much more severe bites — or even an attack one day.

Why? Winning wrestle games makes you the boss of the group. This means if your son and his friends ever show Rover disrespect in the future, then he's earned the right to bite them severely. Bites are the way older dogs teach teenagers respect in the Dog World. Unfortunately, many teenage humans have suffered tragic dog attacks or bites for this reason — especially boisterous, competitive teenage boys.

My advice is to never let anyone wrestle with your dog. Rover's mania for wrestling with human teenagers stops today.

4

Puppies

I suggest you start training your pup from the very first moment you meet it. Why? I believe it's your job to take over the natural training lessons your pup's mammy already started. Think about it. If you don't teach your pup good dog manners, who will?

Puppy training is simple and happens whenever you're around your pup. All you have to do is create a familiar routine for your pup and then patiently show it how to behave in all sorts of situations. This is how your pup will grow up to be a well-behaved dog that needs virtually no training as an adult.

In this section I'll show you how easy natural puppy training can be. I'll also show you how to avoid your new pup growing up into an unruly teenage rebel.

The truth is, your pup's future rests in your hands right now. Are you going to take the time to raise a dog that's easy to live with, or are you going to raise a rude-mannered rebel that believes it's far more important than everyone else?

Believe me, it's so much easier to train a young pup at this impressionable age, rather than later when it's a rebellious teenager or — worse — a mature dog that's been ruling the roost for years!

Scared new puppy

We've just brought our new pup, Hannah, home and she's so nervous! She's been here two hours and she's still terrified. We have to keep pulling her out from under the sofa. She shies away from everyone and she looks absolutely miserable. What do you suggest we do?

It's so daunting for new pups to come to a strange new pack. What Hannah really needs is much less attention from everyone in your family.

I know it's frustrating, but I want you to ignore Hannah for a few hours. She just needs some time alone to absorb this new place and the new humans in it.

This means the kindest thing you can do is leave her under the sofa and organise the building of a simple indoor puppy pen in the corner of your living room or verandah. As soon as you've erected the pen, place Hannah in it. Now leave her completely alone for a few hours.

Go about your normal business around the house as if she's not there. Try not to even look at her, except discreetly. Occasionally give her natural calming signals by raising your chin, turning your head away, yawning slowly and blinking sleepily. You can really exaggerate your yawns. This tells her in a language she can understand, Relax, we're in control.

We know what we're doing. You're completely safe here with us.

After a few hours, you can bring her out of the pen, still giving sleepy, relaxing signals, and sit with her between your feet. Gently rub her behind the ears, and on the head, neck, shoulders and back as you continue giving her those lovely relaxing signals. Don't scare Hannah by staring at her, cuddling her or pulling her face to yours. Just gently rub her head, neck, shoulders and back. Soothingly say her name and murmur 'Good girl' repeatedly.

Each person can have a turn on their own doing this, but allow Hannah a twenty-minute rest between people so she doesn't get too stressed. If you have children, have an adult sit with them and supervise. So she's not overwhelmed, only let one child sit with her at a time.

Although it's tempting to lavish new pups with lots of affection, keep these touching sessions short — say five minutes maximum. When your five minutes are up, put her back in the pen.

With a shy dog like Hannah, increase the time you spend with her each day gradually. This will give her time to know and trust you all. The secret with shy pups is to be patient and not push yourself constantly into their personal space. Your patience will be rewarded when Hannah quickly learns to trust you and your excellent leadership. The good things about shy pups is that when they mature they're often more loyal than boisterous pups.

All pups — even shy ones — are happiest when they're treated as the least important member of the family.

Are you giving your new pup too much attention?

We've had our new puppy, Hector, for a week now and he's getting surprisingly rough and boisterous with us all. We all love him so much, but what are we doing wrong?

This isn't friendly, affectionate behaviour. If your family gives Hector too much attention, he'll quickly get overexcited because he thinks you're all constantly challenging him to play-fight.

If you look at him too much and constantly touch him, it'll keep triggering his natural desire to challenge you back. This is why he jumps up on you, nips, play-attacks your hands and wrists, scratches, trips you up, leans against you and is generally too boisterous.

Hector, however, doesn't find all this play-fighting fun. He's actually becoming very stressed because he can't keep up play-fighting so many different humans every day. Believe me, too much human attention overwhelms pups.

The solution is simple. From now on, I want everyone in your family to stop giving Hector so much attention. You can do this by not staring at him constantly, not touching him every time he passes by and not incessantly calling him over to you. If you want Hector to feel happy and relaxed, then he needs to feel that he's the least important member of your pack. It really is that simple.

Hector also wants to know there's a clear leader around — and that should be you. It's your job to keep an eye on him and make sure no-one accidently gives him too much attention. If you see Hector getting boisterous, you know he's getting stressed. Ask everyone to ignore him for a while.

Once he stops getting all that overwhelming attention, Hector will start feeling settled and safe. His manic, boisterous behaviour will fade away. He'll come and spend time around you, but he won't try to dominate you nonstop. You'll be amazed at how calm pups can be when they feel like the least important member of your pack.

Hector, more than anything, just wants the chance to relax around you. In the Dog World, pups are usually ignored by the rest of the pack for most of the day. They will play in short bouts with their litter mates or with a playful teenage dog. One pup is never the nonstop centre of attention in any dog pack.

How can we calmly give our pup affection?

How can we show Hector affection without triggering all that play-fighting behaviour?

When Hector looks nice and calm, call him over to you by patting the floor with your hands. As he walks over, raise your chin to keep him in a respectful mood. Slowly yawn and sleepily blink to relax him. Don't stare down at him as you touch him, as this will quickly hype him up — instead, gaze sleepily into the middle distance. Rub him soothingly on top of his head, neck and shoulders. Raise your chin if he starts getting overexcited.

The secret with Hector is to only touch him for a few minutes at a time. Any longer and he'll start getting too boisterous. The moment he starts getting silly — for example leaning against you, mouthing your hands or putting a paw on you — send him away by raising your chin, folding your arms and saying 'Enough!'

Do these few things consistently and you'll have a calm, mannerly pup that's an absolute pleasure to be around.

When do you start training a pup?

When do you suggest I start training Jungle, my new pup?

Start Jungle's training the minute you get him. By training, I mean you should carry on doing the job his mammy's already started, which is to teach him basic pup manners every day.

The main thing you're teaching Jungle is that he's the least important member of your family. If he believes he's the least important, then he'll automatically act in a more respectful way to everyone. The easiest way to teach him he's the least important is to give him less attention than everyone else in your family. I know some people will find this very hard to do.

As the leader, it's also your job to pull him back in line when he gets too boisterous and rough, and also to make sure he doesn't nip anyone. You need to show Jungle how to relax when he gets stressed and confused, and ensure he always behaves respectfully around humans by not invading their personal space.

Think about it. A mammy dog doesn't take her litter of pups down to the local park for an obedience class once a week. She teaches them manners and respectful behaviour throughout the day whenever they need it.

Believe me, now is definitely the time to teach your pup polite manners. If you leave all these essential lessons until Jungle's a teenager or an adult, then watch out — your job is going to be so much harder!

Say no to nips

Ouch! My pup Xav really hurts when we're playing and he suddenly nips me. How can I stop him?

From today onwards, I want you to treat your pup's nips as an extremely serious offence. Always end a nip instantly and angrily.

The next time Xav gets overexcited and play-nips you, fold your arms, go very still, raise your chin and fiercely glare down at him from the side of your eyes and give a deep, impressive growl. Be as scary as possible. This growl tells your pup, Stop nipping me RIGHT NOW.

Most pups will stop and wander off for a little while, shaking off the stressful situation. After Xav's had some time alone to think things over, call him back to you by crouching down, swaying from side to side playfully and calling his name in a happy voice.

As he approaches, raise your chin to remind him to treat you with much more respect this time. Yawn slowly to help calm him down and don't excite with any more energetic games.

Xav now has a new rule: absolutely no more nipping humans, even in play.

Help! Xav's still nipping me!

I tried your suggestion of growling at Xav when he nips me, but he just keeps on nipping. Now what do I do?

If Xav insolently continues to nip you, he's basically telling you, So what if you growl at me? How are you going to stop me? He's openly challenging your authority, so be very serious and angry with him. Xav has to learn to respect the leader's growl, or he'll grow up rude and uncontrollable.

This time, pretend to attack Xav as he's nipping you. You're not hurting him physically, of course. You're giving him a short, sharp scare by making your bluff-attack very realistic. For example, the moment he insolently ignores your growl, lean in and bark sharply and fiercely at him: RA-RA-RA-RA-RA-RA! Go for an Oscar-winning scary performance! It will be your intense anger that frightens Xav out of his insolence. Pups know instantly when you really mean it.

Stop bluff-attacking him when he stops nipping you. Give him some time to shake off his shock and allow him to walk away and think about what just happened. After a while, call him back to you in a friendly, playful way, but raise your chin up high as he approaches and act in a calmer manner so he's now much more respectful around you.

If you leave disciplining Xav until he's older, it'll be too late — so stop those nips now!

Why can't I play-fight with my pup?

My little pup King Kong is so cute when I roll him on his back and play-fight with him. He's a well-known guarding breed and it shows — he gets really feisty when we play fight. I've been encouraging him to grab hold of my hands and shake my fingers hard — and you should hear his ferocious little growls! I want him to be an impressive protection dog one day. Have you any other ideas I could try?

Please don't play-fight with your pup! This will not make him into a protection dog; it will only make him grow up to be a dog that has no respect for humans, and no fear of hurting them either.

In my opinion, the days of owning protection dogs trained to attack on command are well and truly over. Such specialised dogs should be only owned by fully trained professionals in the police and armed forces.

An owner-trained backyard protection dog is like owning a loaded gun that could one day seriously hurt innocent people (and other dogs), including members of your own family. It's dangerous enough owning a well-known guarding breed without encouraging him to show even more aggression.

It's definitely time to radically rethink the way you view King Kong. From now on, I want you to start thinking of yourself as your pup's own personal bodyguard. This means it's your job to make sure King Kong grows up to be as safe and unaggressive as possible. It will be your job to make sure he never gets into trouble for showing aggression to anyone.

For a start, teach King Kong to respect you as his leader. If you teach him to maul your hands you're only encouraging him to use aggression to dominate humans, as he's learning from a young age that his teeth can easily win him victories. Every sharp nip he gives you makes him feel even more powerful and dominant. If you continue to play-fight with him, imagine how important he'll think he is by the time he reaches maturity!

When he's older, he won't hesitate to use his teeth to get his own way. He might bite a dog down the street, a member of your own household if they do something he doesn't want them to — or even nip a child walking past your gate.

This means you can't play any more mock-fighting games with him. From today onwards, I want you to teach King Kong the one unbreakable taboo all dogs should learn from their owners: no dog teeth should ever make contact with human skin, even in play.

This taboo will help prevent King Kong from biting someone seriously one day. Please don't encourage your dog to become a deadly weapon.

Motherly love?

The other day I took my five-month-old pup, Pete, back to see his mother for a fun visit. However, we all got a shock when she chased after him and badly attacked him — then walked off and had nothing else to do with him. What on earth happened to motherly love?

Motherly love had nothing to do with it. The reason Mother Dog attacked Pete was because she no longer considers him part of her pack.

Whether she recognised him or not, he was an

intruder that rudely rushed in and started acting in a very disrespectful way around her. Her sharp attack was a quick warning to remember his respectful dog manners around an older dog.

Pups like Pete that don't have an older dog around to teach them polite dog manners usually end up getting bitten by another dog sooner or later. As you've discovered, the behaviour you've been letting Pete get away with at home is obviously unacceptable to other dogs.

Actually, this fight might end up being a good thing for both of you. It's a warning that you've still got more polite manners to teach Pete. So read through this book several times to see what else you have to teach your pup — or Pete's going to get attacked again by some other dog in the future.

If you do need to take Pete back to his mother's property, keep him on a leash and tie him up during the visit — and keep a close eye on him. Better safe than sorry. Pete's mum may have a few more manners she wants to teach him with her teeth!

Warning! Your pup must have turned into a teenager overnight!

Bolly, our six-month-old pup, has been unusually naughty lately. It's such a shame, because we tried some of your ideas a month ago and they settled him down nicely. In fact, no-one could believe what a well-behaved pup he'd become. But in the last week or so he's started to really misbehave again. He's really getting quite cheeky and pushy. What are we doing wrong?

Don't panic, Bolly is just turning into a teenager. Now you're witnessing what hormone surges do to a young dog — they make him want to challenge you nonstop. However, since all dogs go through teenage hormonal surges, all you can do is survive them as best you can.

How long do they last? Expect Bolly to test your leadership a lot until he's about two and a half to three years old. The teenage period is when many dogs go to the pound because they exhaust their owners with their nonstop challenges.

But there are some simple things you can do to help you survive your dog's teenage phase. For a start, make sure you have a strong daily routine to help settle Bolly down. Keep him on a leash more often when indoors and when out in public. Give him two exhausting walks a day. Build him a pen so he can destroy whatever he likes in there, without destroying your possessions. Give him plenty of raw bones to chew.

Most of all, make sure Bolly sees you as his calm, inexhaustible leader. This is when you're really going to be tested by your teenager because he's going to try to overwhelm you with all his extra energy.

He's trying to work out whether you really deserve to be called the boss. All you can do is win as many challenges as you can each day. Good luck!

5

Rescue Dogs

I've always had a soft spot for rescue dogs — probably because I'm a bit of a rescue dog myself.

These days, more and more families are offering a second chance to a dog, usually an adult, that's been given to the protection of the animal-welfare services for a wide range of reasons.

The biggest mistake most people make with rescue dogs is simply giving the new dog far too much attention straightaway. This section will show you how to bring a rescue dog into your household and help it settle in calmly and happily.

Yippee! We're getting a rescue dog!

Our family's so excited — we've decided to go to an animal shelter and adopt a female rescue dog that we're going to call Snoopy! Is there anything special we should know about owning a rescue dog?

Rescue dogs can be wonderful — in fact, all my own dogs are rescue dogs. However, there are several things you should keep in mind when you adopt one.

The secret to making Snoopy well behaved is to not give her very much attention to start with. I know some people will find this very difficult to do — and kids will find it virtually impossible. However, it's very important to always treat your rescue dog as the least important member of your family — even on her first day in your home. If you don't, she will start misbehaving straightaway.

What's the best way to pick her up from the shelter? If possible, have just one person — or at least just the adults — collect Snoopy. A carful of kids will make Snoopy feel totally overwhelmed. Secure her leash so she can't move around in the car, and be very aloof with her on the trip home.

Moving to a new pack is an extremely stressful experience for any dog, so don't overwhelm Snoopy with too much attention straightaway. You can relax her by lifting your chin, slowly yawning and sleepily blinking, and not looking at her. Now you're telling her, I know we're strangers — but you can trust us. You'll be safe with us.

If you keep staring at her, patting her and talking to her — it will seem to Snoopy as though you're trying to challenge her nonstop. Being lavished with lots of affection and attention by strangers is overwhelming and stressful for dogs — so please rein in your human desire to be super-friendly to Snoopy.

What do you do when you get home? Ask everyone to ignore Snoopy and go about their normal business as you take her for a lap of the garden to go to the toilet before you bring her inside or up onto the verandah.

Secure her leash in a corner of the room, give her a mat to sit on and walk away to leave her in peace so she can absorb her new surroundings. Yes, I know everyone wants to start lavishing her with attention — but you're going to overwhelm her if you all close in on poor Snoopy at once.

I suggest your family now sits down to watch a movie together. This will help you act in a naturally relaxed way and will also help stop you all from staring avidly at Snoopy. Ask everyone to ignore her, even if she starts barking. After being ignored for a while she'll lie down and simply watch everyone or even just snooze. If she turns her back on everyone and lies down with her chin on the ground — then congratulations, Snoopy's very politely asking if she can fit into your family. Leave her in peace for now so she has a chance to relax before you sit with her for a pat.

So when do you get to touch her? After an hour or so you can take turns to sit in a chair next to Snoopy. Call her to you. Calmly rub your fingers through the fur on top of her head, and on her neck and shoulders. Always sit in a chair next to her, not on the floor beside her or she'll naturally start challenging you.

As you rub, raise your chin, yawn slowly, blink sleepily and turn your head away to help keep Snoopy relaxed. For now, only sit with her and touch her for a few minutes at a time before calmly walking away, not looking back.

Sit with each of your children when it's their turn so you can oversee them meeting the exciting new dog. You'll have to remind them to keep their chins raised and give Snoopy slow, sleepy relaxing signals. Also remind them not to stare directly at Snoopy — otherwise she'll find their intense gaze very confrontational and she'll start throwing nonstop challenges at them.

Gradually increase the amount of attention you give her over the next few weeks. However, never fall into the trap of giving her too much attention. Until she gets to know you continue to touch her for just a few minutes at a time, as any longer will be stressful for her. Always remember, Snoopy should see herself as the least important member of your family.

When can you give her more freedom? I suggest you keep Snoopy clipped on her leash when you bring her inside for at least two weeks. When she's on the verandah, keep her on the leash when your family sits outside for two weeks as well. Don't let her off the leash around people just yet as she'll naturally start trying to dominate them. This time spent on the leash will help teach her wonderful manners inside and around people. The rest of the time she can spend free in your backyard or in her special dog pen.

Good luck with Snoopy, your new rescue dog!

What do we do if our rescue dog starts to get naughty and noisy?

We brought Danny, our new rescue dog, home today — and we spent plenty of time making him feel welcome. We had great fun patting and playing with him. However, now we can't get him to calm down. He's acting crazy, racing around the house, barking his head off, jumping up on the kids, licking everyone's face, scratching our legs with his claws, and nipping us all in excitement. How can I stop this madness? I'm beginning to wish we never got a rescue dog at all.

What went wrong? I'm afraid you made the mistake of giving Danny far too much attention and freedom on his first day with your family. All Danny's crazy behaviour is actually revealing how stressed he is. You can tell this by his frantic, noisy behaviour, the way he's trying to dominate everyone, the way he's nervously panting, and the way he rushes from one person to the next.

Dogs get really stressed by human chaos. When Danny became overwhelmed by all the nonstop pats and staring eyes of your family — who are, after all, complete strangers to him — he realised he had to quickly win control of everyone. This is why he started desperately throwing challenges at everyone so he could dominate you all. He started dominantly barking, jumping up, licking, scratching and nipping.

How can you calm him down? Give poor Danny some peace and quiet alone so he can settle down and absorb his new surroundings and his new pack.

I suggest you make one adult the boss in charge of Danny so he doesn't get confused about who he should obey. I'll assume the boss is you. Clip Danny on a leash and secure him in a corner of the room with a mat to sit on so he's out of everyone's way.

Now ask your family to ignore the dog and act as though he's invisible. The best way they can do this is to go about their normal business around the house or sit down together and watch a movie. Not being watched, touched or talked to is going to help settle down poor, stressed, overexcited Danny.

As Danny's leader you can give him regular relaxing signals — raise your chin and give really slow, sleepy yawns and blinks as you turn your head away from him. Ignore any stressed barking — eventually he'll mimic everyone else's relaxed attitude and lie down to snooze.

What happens if he won't stop barking? If he really won't settle down quietly he's having trouble ridding himself of the stress caused by the earlier chaos. The best thing you can do is take him for a walk on the leash at least around the block — but ideally for a really good, exhausting distance. In fact, I've found a great way for your whole family to bond with a new rescue dog is to take it on a leash for a good, long walk together.

In this way Danny gets to walk off the stress of moving to a new house and meeting a whole group of strangers. He also feels as if he's genuinely part of your pack. Even better, he'll be nicely exhausted for his first night in a strange house.

How can we survive our rescue dog's first night?

I'm a bit concerned about tonight — our first night with Tigger, our new rescue dog. One of my friends warned me the first night he had his new rescue dog it was a complete nightmare: the dog barked all night; it ran around the house, making a mess; and it went to the toilet inside. Have you any suggestions about how to stop our first night with Tigger becoming a nightmare too?

Your first night with a rescue dog certainly doesn't have

to be a nightmare. All you need to do is follow these few simple suggestions.

Make sure no-one gives Tigger too much attention. If he's overwhelmed with lots of strangers trying to touch him, stare at him, talk to him and play with him, he's going to get very stressed. If he gets too stressed he's going to find it very difficult to settle down later when you want him to go to sleep quietly.

On the other hand, the more you ignore Tigger on his first day, the more he'll relax in his new home. You're not being cruel — you're just giving him breathing space and a chance to observe his strange new surroundings in peace. He can still spend time around you — just stop trying to interact with him nonstop.

Get Tigger used to being tied up. Make sure Tigger can be safely secured on a leash when he's brought inside. Some dogs need to learn to accept the leash because they've never been tied up before. The best time to teach Tigger this is when you bring him inside in the evening while you're relaxing and watching TV. For the best results, make sure he's exhausted from an earlier long walk.

Calmly clip Tigger on his leash, bring him inside and secure his leash so he can't move far off the mat you've put down for him in a corner of the living room. Now you can keep an eye on him and sort out any problems with the leash before bedtime. After you've secured his leash so he can't move far off his mat, walk away. Watch TV instead of your new rescue dog to help him 'switch off'.

Tigger should be so tired from his walk that he soon lies down when you ignore him and, hopefully, he'll snooze off. If he does this, just leave him alone and don't disturb him.

If Tigger struggles and pulls away from the leash, relax him by turning your head away with your chin raised and giving him plenty of slow yawns as you sleepily blink. This may even take twenty minutes or so. The calmer and sleepier you get, the more he'll mimic you.

If he starts dominantly barking to be let off, raise your chin, growl in warning at him and barge through him until he's quiet. Unfortunately, you didn't give him enough exercise earlier.

Ideally your dog should be snoozing for about three hours in your living room before you put him to bed.

Keep Tigger on a leash when he's around people and other animals. If you do this whenever Tigger's inside your home or outside your property he won't get the opportunity to win many challenges against everyone. This will automatically put him in a more submissive mood. Submissive dogs are quiet, well-behaved dogs.

Tigger can have freedom off the leash when you let him out into your backyard or put him in his pen on his own. However, if you allow Tigger to run around dominating everyone all day, then good luck expecting him to behave quietly later that night! He's going to keep trying to dominate everyone by racing around barking all night.

Exhaust Tigger with at least one long walk on the leash. My motto with rescue dogs (and any dogs) is 'A really tired dog is a really well-behaved dog'. Keep in mind, too, that Tigger may be desperate for exercise when he leaves the rescue shelter. He may have been cooped up in a pen for weeks. You can't expect him to sleep well on his first night if he's jumping out of his skin in need of exercise.

Bedtime. I believe your dog will sleep better inside the safety of your inner den — which is the inside of your house. Decide on a good place to let him sleep: perhaps in the laundry on a secured leash? Never give a rescue dog the run of your house, as he may destroy it. Even if he doesn't, too much freedom inside the important inner-den area will make him feel far too important.

Finally, when it's time to put Tigger to bed, calmly yawn as you take him on his leash through to the laundry. Act as sleepy as possible; sleepiness is so contagious! Bring his mat in as this will make Tigger feel secure.

Secure Tigger so he can comfortably curl up on his bedding. Give him more relaxing, sleepy signals as you raise your chin and calmly walk out of the room. Don't hug him or make a fuss of him.

If you're nervous about leaving Tigger tied up, leave him loose in your laundry but make sure he can't escape. Be aware, however, that he may chew and destroy the contents. Make sure there are no poisons or electrical cords Tigger can get hold of.

If Tigger's exhausted enough by that earlier walk he'll definitely just want to sniff around and then curl up and fall asleep. Moving to a new house full of strangers is a very exhausting experience.

First thing in the morning, take Tigger outside to go to the toilet.

These are all great ways to survive your first night with your new rescue dog!

When do we start training our rescue dog?

We brought our new dog Nellie home from the rescue shelter today and she's sweet but quite undisciplined and very pushy. She could certainly do with some training. When do you think we should start?

Start training your new rescue dog the minute you meet her! As you've already had Nellie a few hours she's probably had plenty of opportunities to score challenges from everyone. This is why she's already misbehaving. From now on, try not to lose any more challenges to her.

This is why I want you to keep Nellie on a leash whenever she comes inside or is around people for at least the first week. If she's secured on a leash there are very few challenges she can win. Think about it. If Nellie's on a leash inside she can't rush around dominating anyone by jumping up, licking, nipping and demanding pats, and she can't run around your house causing damage and mess.

Don't let her bark. About the only thing Nellie can do when she's on a leash is bark in protest, shouting out, LET ME GO! LET ME GO!

If she does this, try to relax her by ignoring her, turning your back on her, and looking as sleepy as possible. Yawn slowly with your chin raised. If this doesn't settle Nellie down after ten minutes or so, she's too stressed to relax. Nellie may be barking because she still feels restless from being cooped up in her caged pen at the shelter. Most dogs start misbehaving after only two days without a good walk, yet Nellie may have been without a proper walk for several weeks. No wonder she's having trouble settling down now.

So take Nellie for a long, exhausting walk on the leash to get rid of all her pent-up energy. I wouldn't take her off the leash out in public for at least three weeks. If you do this before she's convinced you're her boss, just watch how much she'll misbehave! She'll notch up a big score of challenges against you. She may also run off as the ultimate challenge. So keep that leash on until you can trust her.

When you return home from your nice, long walk, keep her on the leash and put her to bed. Ignore her as soon as she settles down to snooze. Once she's tired, she won't bark. Always remember that great saying — a tired dog is a quiet dog!

When can Nellie come off the leash indoors? You'll be the best judge of when she can be trusted to be free indoors. If she's a submissive sort of dog you can try giving her gradual freedom inside after only a week. If she's a stubborn, pushy dog I'd wait until she's more respectful before giving her the run of your house. Never let a misbehaving, dominant dog have too much freedom inside or you'll soon end up in chaos.

What's the best time of the day to train Nellie? It doesn't matter what time of the day or night it is — if Nellie throws a challenge at you, deal with it. Treat every day as a training day until she learns polite manners. The best way you can do this is by reading through this book so you know which challenges you have to work on. Then gradually win as many challenges as you can each day.

If you lose a challenge, don't get into a pointless argument with her — just work out how to win it next time.

The idea is to gradually win more and more challenges in a calm, inexhaustible way.

After about three weeks of you winning enough challenges, Nellie should see you as her boss. If she's a pushy personality, expect her to take a little longer. Once she sees you as her boss, you'll have a polite, well-mannered dog who really likes being with you.

6

More than One

Many people get a shock when they add another dog to their household and quickly find themselves submerged in noisy, aggressive chaos. This section shows you how to keep dog politics to a minimum by introducing a simple hierarchy system. This is the natural way peace and order are kept in the Dog World.

Puppy Invasion Day

Doc is our old dog and he reacted in a really horrible way yesterday when we brought our new pup, Lucy, home. He growled at her when she bounced over to say hello, and he nearly attacked her a few times when she tried to follow him around and make friends. In fact, he's scaring us by the intense way he dislikes her. Lucy's so sweet — how could Doc hate her? We thought Doc would love having a new dog for company. How can we help them get along better?

Doc and Lucy are only going to get along when you start treating one dog as more important than the other. You must decide which dog is going to be your Number One dog.

As no old dog is going to accept being subservient to a pup, the more important dog should be Doc. This means that from now on, Doc gets more attention than Lucy, he gets patted first, he gets fed before her and he gets the best bed.

I know it's hard not to lavish all your attention on your exciting new pup, but if you keep doing it, Doc will have no alternative but to discipline Lucy by nipping or even attacking her. As the higher ranking dog, Doc has every right to teach this young pup her place.

However, if things get out of hand, clip both dogs on secured leashes until they settle down.

Please be aware that it's usually humans who upset the natural politics of dogs. They do this by giving the wrong dog too much attention — and this quickly triggers a fight. However, you'll have no problems if everyone — including your visitors — always treats Doc as more important than Lucy.

Don't worry, once you've treated Lucy as the less-important dog for a few weeks, Doc will gradually come to like and trust her!

Brotherly love?

I bought two brother pups from the same litter and now it's a nightmare! Ross and Stuart are now two years old and are constantly at each other's throats. I don't know how to stop them fighting. Ross seems to be the bigger, pushier dog. What do you suggest?

The breeder should have advised you not to buy two pups from the same litter. As your two brothers are maturing, they're fighting to work out pack order. Here are some ideas to stop them fighting.

Make Ross your Number One dog. As the leader, you can stop most of the fighting if you decide which should be the more dominant dog. As Ross is the pushier of the two, treat him as more important than Stuart. This means that from now on you must always feed Ross first, pat him first, give him more attention, talk to him more and give him the best bed.

Feeding Ross his evening meal is particularly important. This is the main time of the day when you, the leader, show everyone who your Number One dog is. This is why feeding time can get very political for dogs; if you feed the wrong dog first you'll get an instant fight.

Create a dinner routine. To avoid the evening meal triggering a fight you have to prove you're in calm control. To do this, before you feed them, tether both dogs on secured leashes, with a decent distance between them. Ask each dog to sit before you feed it.

Feed Ross first. Pretend to nibble from his bowl, pull a disgusted face and say, 'Yuk!', and drop the bowl at his feet. Now your dog believes you're only giving him your unwanted leftovers. This is a great way to remind your Number One dog that he's still less important than you.

Now feed Stuart in the same way. When both dogs are finished and nicely calm, you can unclip their leashes. Leave them to digest their food in peace.

I suggest you feed your dogs any raw bones in the same way. Afterwards, pick up any scraps before you unclip them so they can't find any bones of contention.

Clip each dog to his own bed of an evening. Dogs fight over beds, so take control of these too, otherwise you might have a fight break out in the middle of the night as one dog tries to steal the other dog's bed.

The easiest way to stop fights over beds is for you to decide which bed Ross gets. This will be the best bed.

Now clip your dogs on secured leashes every evening so they can only reach their own bed. After a week or so — both dogs will get used to sleeping on their own beds and you can gradually start unclipping them from their bed leashes as you trust them more.

Remove fight-starters. I want you to remove anything that could trigger a fight between Ross and Stuart. For example, don't leave bowls of dry food around for them to fight over. Don't let them have any toys or balls. Don't give them a hanging tyre to play with. I also suggest you don't play any more competitive games with them for a while — if ever again. Games like fetching sticks and balls can often trigger a fight as your dogs' adrenaline starts pumping.

Tie up both dogs when you go out. To avoid any trouble breaking out when you're not at home, I suggest you always secure each dog in his own pen or on his own leash when you go out. Some dogs may use your absence to try to start a fight. When the leader's away, the followers may erupt into a civil war!

When you have visitors over, secure each dog separately. This is because most visitors cause tension for dogs — and if there's any tension in the air, your two dogs are going to want to fight.

Don't allow any more fighting. I want you to develop zero tolerance for fights. When your dogs fight they're both openly challenging your authority. No leader dog would accept it, so neither should you. The minute you hear any sort of aggression — even a growl — I want you to stand tall and growl at both dogs then go and clip them on their leashes, secured near each other but safely out of reach.

If they still growl at each other on the leashes — but as long as they don't show aggression to you — march straight over to the worst offender and raise your chin as you barge straight through him. As your dog moves away to give you ground you're telling him that you're the leader and he has no authority to start a fight. Repeat with the other dog.

Once both dogs are giving you polite, submissive signals, such as stepping smoothly out of your way, putting their ears and tails down low, and being quiet, you can walk away and let them think about things.

Unfortunately, I've found that some brothers will always fight once they reach maturity no matter what you do. This will happen if they both have such dominant personalities that neither dog will be submissive. If this is the case with Ross and Stuart, I'm afraid you're going to have to find one of them a new home before they kill each other.

Dogs that erupt into fights are too dangerous to live together. They could have a serious fight when you're not at home. You'll be constantly taking them to the vet to get stitched up. Worse — someone could get hurt trying to break them up.

All you can learn from this experience is never to get brothers from the same litter again. Brotherly love isn't necessarily guaranteed in the Dog World. Remember, these two brothers have been competing with each other since birth — when they had to fight for their mammy's teat!

Why do my two dogs trash my house when I go out?

Help! My two young dogs Mitch and Dusty completely destroy anything they can get their teeth into when I go out. Are they mad at me for leaving them behind? They look so guilty when I return and shout at them for causing such devastation. Please help me come up with a solution — they're costing me a fortune!

I suspect Mitch and Dusty actually have the time of their lives when you go out! When you leave two such energetic dogs alone they will play together for hours, challenging each other with nonstop games.

The trouble is, playing together in this way triggers their natural predator behaviour of 'tear, shake and kill'. So Mitch and Dusty pretend shoes and cushions — and whatever else they can find — are prey animals. With great excitement, they work as a team to wrestle and yank each piece of 'prey' between themselves as they practice all their instinctive hunting moves. This kind of play is a fun way to work off their excess energy, but ultimately such games decide which dog is the more dominant. So to answer your question, Mitch and Dusty aren't angry at you for leaving them at home; they are just playing games together that accidently destroy your things.

The 'guilt' you see on your return home is also instinctive. Both dogs can tell by your voice, body language, smell and energy that you're genuinely angry and distressed, and they're trying to display the most submissive body language they can. This is the way dogs instinctively try to switch off a higher-ranking dog's anger, so they don't get attacked.

What's the solution? You'll never stop young dogs from playing games together, and it would be cruel to try. The only answer is to provide Mitch and Dusty with their own Dog Land, a place where they can play their games and where it doesn't matter what kind of damage they cause. This is why I believe dog pens are so invaluable. Let Mitch and Dusty happily play their boisterous games in a secure pen they can't escape from. Give them balls, branches, rags and bits of rope in this pen to use as pretend prey animals.

Young dogs need to play. It's up to you as their leader to provide a suitable place where they can.

Food wars

My two dogs Noel and Doyle have started having serious fights while they're eating. What do you suggest? Noel is the pushier dog and usually starts each fight.

Noel and Doyle need to learn new manners around food. Whenever your dogs start arguing between themselves, take control by calmly clipping each dog on their own long leash and keeping them well out of reach of each other. This sends a clear message to them: I'm in control here and as your leader I say there's to be absolutely NO fighting in this pack, ever.

If your dogs aren't aggressive to you, reinforce this message by barging through each of them until they're submissively stepping back out of your way, with both of them yawning and blinking. Once they're giving these submissive signals, they're showing that they respect your authority.

Clip Noel and Doyle on secured leashes for all meals. Don't get lazy about taking this basic safety precaution; the alternatives are an expensive vet's bill and plenty of dog stitches!

Both dogs should be able to see each other, but should be secured far apart. However, if they still show aggression towards each other, move their leashes so they eat out of sight of each other.

To put an end to all fights in the future, it's essential to ensure both dogs respect you as the leader at mealtime. Here's a great way to do this. Once each dog is clipped onto its own leash, feed Noel first, since he seems to be the more dominant of the two. But before you give Noel his meal, get him to sit submissively for you. Pretend to nibble the food, then pull a disgusted face and say, 'Yuk!', to show you're only giving him your unwanted leftovers. Then drop the bowl at his feet and immediately walk away to let him eat in peace. Then do the same for Doyle. Yes, as petty as it seems, always do things for Noel, the more dominant dog, first.

Ten minutes later, come and take their bowls away, then return and release the dogs. I believe you should leave dogs alone after a meal so their food can be digested. If there's any aggression at all, clip both dogs back on their leashes until they settle down again. From now on, I want you to develop zero tolerance to any signs of aggression from your dogs. At the first growl, clip them back on their leashes.

One last thing: I suggest you never trust these dogs to feed peacefully together off their leashes. This means you can't leave dry food around for your dogs to nibble at during the day. Also, I'd always clip the dogs on their leashes when you feed them bones; don't let the bones become bones of contention!

Senseless barking

Please help me before I go deaf! My two little dogs Jed and Dylan constantly race around my house barking noisily at each other. How can I stop this horrible noise?

Jed and Dylan are using all that barking noise to try to dominate each other. It's like a never-ending noise contest with no clear winner. Your dogs are being treated as equals by you, so now they're using this noise contest to try to work out which should rank higher than the other.

What can you do to stop the noise? Develop zero tolerance to any more barking on your property — and especially inside your house. If you hear either dog bark, yap, or even murmur softly, march angrily straight towards the offender, glare down at him from the corner of your eye, growl in warning and say, 'Enough!'

If the offender keeps barking, barge straight through him until he gives way to your authority and stops his barking.

If both dogs race away and keep barking, clip them on leashes in different corners of the room and give each a mat to relax on.

Remember, you're the leader of the inside of your house; it's your right to have a serene inner den to relax in. I want you to start recognising that any barking whatsoever inside this important area is an open challenge to your leadership. So barge through both dogs as often as you need to until they stay respectfully quiet.

I also suggest you help calm down both dogs by using relaxing signals. Once they stop barking, ignore them completely and raise your chin as you go about your normal business. Every now and again, slowly yawn and sleepily blink as you turn your head away from them.

If either dog insolently starts barking again, use the barge-through technique again, even when they're clipped on their leashes. Very soon you'll have a much quieter house. You can unclip your dogs once they're behaving in a quiet, respectful manner.

However, you also have to sort out the reason Jed and Dylan are having barking contests in the first place. As the leader, you must decide which dog should have the higher rank.

Let's assume the naturally more dominant dog is Jed. Make him your Number One dog. This means you have to always treat him as being more important than Dylan. You can do this by always feeding Jed first. Whoever gets their dinner first is always considered the more dominant dog. You can also help Jed feel he's more dominant than Dylan by giving him everything first — and the best of everything. For example, always pat Jed first. Always give him treats first. Give him the best bed. Give him more attention ... You get the idea.

Believe me, these ranking politics mean everything to dogs. If you have two dogs, one dog should always be treated more importantly than the other — otherwise you'll have nonstop drama.

Dogs hate being treated as equals by humans because it just causes so much confusion. Remember, there's no such thing as equality in the Dog World. If you start treating Jed and Dylan as equals, then they'll have to resort back to playing their noisy barking contest again.

By the way, visitors can upset the natural order within minutes, so keep an eye on what's happening when your friends come over. I suggest you ask your visitors to ignore the dogs, or remove Jed and Dylan to their pen.

Well, Jed and Dylan, your unnecessary noise contest ends today. We've worked out a better way to decide who's more dominant — Jed just gets fed his dinner first!

May the best dog win

When our two dogs play energetic chasing games, Spot usually gives up first and flops down on the ground, panting and exhausted. Then Jet walks over and stands over him, quite still. Only after Spot puts his chin on the ground does Jet, the winner, walk off. What's this all about?

When Jet stands over Spot in this way, he's saying, I won that game. Admit defeat or I'll assume you're challenging my leadership.

By placing his chin on the ground, Spot's telling him, Okay … I admit defeat. You won that game.

Such standover poses help to show which is the more dominant dog without having to resort to a dog fight.

Old Jay's wisdom

My old dog, Jay, never seems to want to play with our younger dog, Georgie. Why do you think this is?

Old dogs like Jay are wise enough not to play games that are too energetic with younger dogs. Remember, if you win the game, you also win the right to be in charge. Old dogs know very well that it's far too easy to be toppled from their high ranking by a fitter, more energetic young dog that can win plenty of games.

When Georgie, a young challenger, invites Jay, an old dog, to join in a game by frisking about, Jay may just lift his chin and wander off in a bored, aloof way as though such silly games are beneath him. But the reality is your older dog knows he has a good chance of losing. No old dog is going to risk losing his more dominant position to a younger dog over something as stupid as a game.

If Georgie keeps pushily hassling old Jay to play with him, he'll get nipped sharply. When this happens, don't reprimand him. Jay has every right to put Georgie, the ambitious young challenger, in his place.

As I've said before, games are taken very seriously in the Dog World. They help decide who the real boss is.

Help your old dog win respect

I have an older dog, Molly, and a younger energetic dog, Bluey. This younger dog tortures Molly by constantly bugging her to play games. Poor old Molly keeps trying to walk away but young Bluey won't stop following her around, hassling her to play. What do you suggest I do?

Young Bluey can't help trying to get Molly to play games with him. Teenage dogs instinctively need to play games. They want to practice all their clever moves and tricks, so they can win play-fights and games. Being a teenager, Bluey also has masses of hormones rushing through him — and far too much energy that needs an outlet.

But make no mistake, Bluey's very aware of what he's doing when he hassles Molly. Every time he friskily demands a game with your older dog, he's saying, Aha, Old Molly, I can see you're losing your grip on the leadership ... look at you: you're getting old, you're avoiding playing my games because you know you'll lose and I'll topple you from your throne. Hey! Maybe I should topple you right now ... come on ... PLAY WITH ME! PLAY WITH ME! COME ON, OLD MOLLY, PLAY WITH ME!

It's your job as a good leader to protect Molly from the rude demands of a pushy young dog like Bluey. The easiest way you can protect her is by simply giving her more freedom than Bluey.

So while Molly can freely snooze around the lawn and inside your house, keep Bluey in the dog pen when you aren't around to supervise him, or clip him on a long, secured leash. Now Molly can easily escape from him if she wants to. You could also give over-energetic Bluey some bones to keep him occupied, and increase his daily exercise. Your new goal is to keep Bluey constantly exhausted.

If you don't give Molly these well-deserved holidays from Bluey, you'll see her get hassled into an early grave. Believe me, you'll literally watch her age. An older dog's muzzle quickly turns white when there's a pushy, exhausting teenage dog around.

After all the years of loyalty Molly's given you, doesn't she deserve your help to keep this boisterous teenager Bluey under control?

Hey, youngster! What's that I hear out there?

Something strange has been going on lately between my two dogs. Dominic is our older boss dog, and Sandy is our young, pushy teenage dog. If young Sandy runs inside and steals Dominic's bed, Dominic stands over him, pauses, then runs outside barking his head off. Next minute Sandy's racing after him, barking his head off too. When Dominic returns first and climbs onto to his own bed, he acts as though nothing unusual happened. These manic bursts of barking and racing outside are driving me demented. Why are they doing it — and how can I stop them?

Aah ... you have to admire a wise old dog like Dominic. He's using a clever tactic to win back his own bed from the ambitious youngster, Sandy, who stole it. Let's see how he won his precious bed back without a fight.

Old Dominic came over and found Sandy had stolen his bed. Having the best bed is very important in the Dog World — and the highest ranking dog will always want it. Having the best bed shows everyone how high your position is within the pack. Whenever young Sandy tries to steal Dominic's bed, he's saying to your older dog, Ha ha! I got here first, so I deserve this, not you.

Dominic then walks to Sandy and stands very still over him, telling him, Don't test me. That bed's mine. Now give it back.

By not moving, Sandy was insolently saying, Yeah? Make me.

Now Dominic has to decide what to do. Start a dog fight? Not a great idea because he could lose against a young dog like Sandy. Instead, he wisely decides to use his brains to get Sandy off his bed.

He pretends to hear something unusual happening outside, so he stands and looks as if he's listening and concentrating, then suddenly he barks loudly to alert everyone that he hears intruders. Now he races outside in a very convincing performance to chase off those imaginary intruders.

His barks are telling Sandy, Come on, youngster ... I can hear there's something out there — quick! It must be intruders! Come on, help me investigate!

The moment Sandy, the younger and faster dog, races ahead, Dominic thinks, Hee hee! That youngster's run far enough ahead for me to whip back inside and grab my own bed again.

As you can see, Dominic might be getting on in years but there are plenty of tricks left in your old dog yet. However, the problem with Dominic's clever tactic is that you end up with lots of noisy bursts of barking and frantic races, so you, the leader, have to sort out once and for all who owns which bed.

There's an easy way to do this. Put the beds away during the day until you have the issue sorted. Have two sturdy wall hooks installed, one near the usual location of each bed. In the evening, put the beds out again, but clip both dogs on leashes and secure each to the wall hook nearest their bed. Make sure you give Dominic, the older dog, the bed he prefers. Now each dog can only lie on his own bed.

After the dogs have been being clipped to their beds for a few evenings while you watch TV, you can then unclip Dominic. However, keep cheeky Sandy clipped on his bed leash for another few days — or until he learns to be more respectful towards Dominic. If the noisy politics start up again, don't hesitate to clip Sandy back on his leash.

It will also help if everyone in your family always treats old Dominic as being much more important than Sandy. For example, make sure you always feed Dominic his dinner first. Always pat Dominic first and give him much more attention. This will stop Sandy feeling important enough to challenge old Dominic by stealing his bed.

Now as Dominic watches you clip Sandy on his bed leash, he'll gratefully think, Thanks, Boss, for sorting out that cheeky youngster Sandy for me.

7

The Boss of the Walk

Becoming the boss of the walk is the battle all dominant dogs love to win. This is because if you win the battle of wills out on the walk, then you also win the right to do whatever you want out in public.

In this section I'll help you win this very important battle of wills step by step, so your walks will stop being such a nightmare. Remember, you adopted a dog to enjoy, not do daily battle with.

The daily hunt

Why does my dog Dino get so excited and strain at the leash when we set off for a walk? Is he just glad to get out and about?

When you take Dino for his daily walk he thinks you're actually taking him out on the daily hunt! He looks forward all day to those walks. Dino's instincts are all fired up and his adrenaline is pumping. This is why he has all that energy and excitement as you leave the house.

Sometimes all that excited energy makes it much more difficult to walk him, especially in mild, cool weather — perfect hunting conditions. Good hunting conditions are also why dogs naturally prefer being walked in the early mornings and late afternoons — when prey is most likely to be around, foraging. Dino doesn't care that you never actually catch anything — why should he worry? You always provide food for him later!

Now you know Dino sees his daily walk as the daily hunt, keep it in mind when you're deciding whether to clip him on a leash — especially when you walk around the streets of suburbia. Your dog has automatically switched into hunt mode; are you really prepared to give Dino complete freedom with so many distractions around? His mind is only thinking of one thing: the hunt! What happens if something prey-like crosses his path; will you be able to stop him following his instincts?

The twice-a-day rule

How often should I walk my dog Cormac? He's pretty energetic because he's a teenager.

Unless your vet recommends otherwise, I believe dogs are happier and better behaved when they get two walks a day, every day.

The best times to walk Cormac are in the morning and again in the afternoon. These are the natural hunting and scent-marking times for dogs when Cormac will have a natural craving to leave your property.

Some people hope that their backyard is like some sort of exercise machine for their dog. The truth is, your backyard is incredibly boring for Cormac. The two daily walks you give him are the real highlights of his day.

If you don't walk Cormac at least once every single day you'll see behaviour problems appear very quickly. Walking is one of the major responsibilities — and pleasures — of owning a dog. I get saddened by the thought of all the dogs around the world abandoned in their backyards, never getting out for an interesting daily walk.

You also have to ensure that Cormac is getting enough exercise for his breed and age. If he's a herding or sporting breed, then you're going to have to walk him until he's tired. Since Cormac's a teenager, he needs even more exercise. I find swimming exhausts even the fittest dogs.

Believe me, teenage dogs have to be exercised off your property every day without fail. Otherwise all that extra energy gets diverted into misbehaviour as they challenge everyone around them for the leadership.

There's an old saying — and it's so true — a tired dog is a well-behaved dog!

Two walks a day is a great way to tire out an energetic dog like Cormac. But keep in mind: if he's not lazing around your home between those two walks, then he's not getting enough exercise yet!

Are you winning the battle of the walk?

My new dog Emma is a real hassle to walk. The whole experience is totally unenjoyable. What am I doing wrong? I never had this problem with my last dog.

If Emma is a naturally pushy dog, the daily walk can quickly turn into a daily battle for supremacy. Believe me, dominant dogs really look forward to this daily clash of wills.

A dog walk is made up of many little challenges that very dominant dogs like Emma find easy to win. If she wins most of these, she gets to be the Boss of the Walk.

Once she's the boss, she never has to obey you out in public — and perhaps even when she returns home. As you are discovering, such dogs are extremely difficult and unenjoyable to walk.

I'm going to help you recognise all the challenges that Emma is throwing at you out on walks. Even better, I'm also going to show you how to start winning them. Although these tests might seem quite petty to us, to dogs they're a very important way of winning power over you. But if you can turn the tables and make yourself Boss of the Walk, Emma will accept your authority and become a pleasure to take out. You'll be amazed at how much her behaviour will improve.

Does your dog run riot when the leash comes out?

My dog Rusty goes crazy when the leash comes out. He gets so excited and jumps around so much, it's like trying to catch a rabbit. I try to clip the leash on as quickly as possible but we usually end up in a shambles. What's a better way of clipping on his leash?

This is what Rusty thinks when he sees you get the leash out: Yippeeee! I love winning this challenge. If I prove I'm really difficult to put the leash on, then I win! It's a great way to win control of the walk before we even step out the gate.

The best thing you can do to solve this frustrating problem is to really start relaxing.

So become the exact opposite of riot-loving Rusty. Get his leash, go and sit down in a chair and let all the air out of your lungs as you make a sleepy, sighing, 'Phwoooooooph!' sound. Blink, yawn slowly and lift your chin in a nonchalant way.

If Rusty continues to riot, lift your chin higher, fold your arms and keep yawning. Look up at the ceiling as if you're watching fluffy white clouds drifting past slowly. Ignoring Rusty as though he doesn't exist is a really effective way of taking back control from him.

From now on, have a new motto: While you're causing chaos and noise I'm going to stop what I'm doing and ignore you. I refuse to be rushed along by your rudeness.

When he settles down again, call him to you and raise your chin as he approaches to remind him you're the boss. Command him to 'Sit!' before you clip his leash on. Keep him sitting by repeating the command 'Stay!'

Only when he's calmly and quietly sitting, do you stand up. Only after he stays sitting politely for you, do you head for the front door with him walking submissively behind you.

If at any stage Rusty starts mucking up again, stop, relax, and go back to your chair. Lean back, fold your arms and start watching those fluffy white clouds drift across the ceiling again. Do this every time he tries misbehaving in any way. Only progress with the walk if he's acting with beautiful, polite manners.

Rusty may continue to test you for a few weeks, but never allow yourself to be hurried along. He'll soon figure out that there will be no walk until he's treating you with respect.

Does your dog race to the door ahead of you on the walk?

As soon as I clip Patsy's leash on and head for the front door, she turns into a lunatic, almost choking herself as she drags me behind her. What's her big rush — and how can I stop her?

Patsy's race to the door is an open challenge to you. In the Dog World, the first one through the important front door wins the right to be Boss of the Walk.

So how do we make sure we win this important challenge? From now on, always make sure you calmly step through the front door with Patsy submissively behind you. This will be easy if you teach her a new habit of walking behind you all the way through the house to the front door.

How? Keep Patsy's leash short and your chin raised. Every time she tries to overtake you, say, 'Back!', as you barge into her. Patsy will quickly learn to submissively walk behind you, even on a loose leash.

When you reach the door with her still behind you, get her to submissively sit. From now on have an unbreakable rule: Patsy's only allowed to walk through that door behind you, whether she's on or off her leash.

Say, 'Back!', and walk through the door with Patsy behind you. Barge her if she tries to dive around you. Practice until she's walking very respectfully behind you back and forth through the door.

If Patsy's still overexcited, command her to sit for you constantly. This will quickly put her in a more submissive mood. Relaxing your body language and raising your chin will help you become more in control of the situation.

Walk more and more slowly so Patsy learns not to rudely overtake you, no matter what. With a bit of practice you should have her obediently staying behind you through that door, even on a loose leash. So make sure you win the race for the front door — but always at a leader's beautiful, sedate pace.

Stair-tripping Trixie

My beautiful little dog Trixie keeps tripping me over on the stairs every time we set off for a walk. I've fallen and bruised my knees a few times and once nearly fell on Trixie. Have you any suggestions?

Trixie is trying to control the walk by deliberately tripping you over. In the Dog World it's always a race to get to the bottom of any stairs first. If you can trip your over opponent on the way down so they're knocked out of the race, then all the better! Fortunately, this is a simple problem to fix; you just have to stop Trixie feeling as if she must win this race at all costs.

Start by changing the overall mood of the dog walk. From now on, the walk should be seen as a very calm experience, with you as the leader who's completely in control. You especially need to prove you're in complete control of every step taken down the stairs.

So let's start making this walk down the staircase a much more relaxed affair.

Before the walk begins, slow your breathing down to deep breaths that will naturally relax you. Bend down and call Trixie to you calmly, blinking slowly. As she reaches you, lift your chin and say, 'Sit.' Clip her leash on and stand up, slowly yawning.

Now take the time to wander around the area at the top of the stairs. You're not stepping down them until Trixie is calmly and submissively walking behind you in the 'Back' position.

This is a great opportunity to use one of my favourite tricks to distract and relax a dog. As you wander around, calmly holding the leash, pause every now and again to pick up objects around the hall and landing. Pretend to be totally engrossed as you leisurely examine them.

Now Trixie will stop thinking, Quick! Stairs! Stairs! Stairs! Stairs! Instead, she'll begin to wonder, Huh? What's my human doing now? This seems interesting. Suddenly those stairs don't seem so important any more.

Once Trixie's behaviour is calmer, wander towards the stairs, more relaxed than ever. If she restarts her excited behaviour, go back to wandering around, pretending to examine those objects again. Be patient, it's worth it.

When Trixie's calm, get her into the habit of sitting at the top of the stairs, staying in the 'Back' position behind you all the way down and sitting again once you reach the bottom. Any dancing and excited shenanigans are to be met with a raised chin and a firm 'Sit', no matter where you happen to be on the stairs. You can remind Trixie to relax by stopping to pull an object out of your pocket and examine it. She'll soon learn that only calm behaviour will get her to the bottom of the stairs.

Let there be no more dangerous tripping down the stairs with Trixie.

Does your dog barge through the gate ahead of you?

As soon as I head for the gate my dog Argus starts to pick up the pace and I know what's going to happen next — he's going to barge through the gate in front of me. I tell him not to, but it's as though he's switched his ears off and he just barges past me anyway. I can't take much more of this. He's a big, strong dog and all that barging hurts.

This is simple bully behaviour. It shows no respect. Argus is sending you a clear message: Get out of my way! I'm the leader — so I go through the gate first.

The reason the front gate is so important to dogs is because it marks the entrance to our territory. Argus knows that if he gets through that gate first, then he earns the right to be Boss of the Walk.

By the way, you'll find if you've got an audience watching, your dog will put some extra argy-bargy into his barging. He'll do this to show everyone watching that he's the leader — both inside the territory and out of it as well. Other dogs especially will notice this dominant behaviour. So if there's another dog's around, expect more barging than usual.

So what's the solution? It's time to make yourself the boss of the gate. First, establish that this is your gate. Tether your dog nearby so he can watch you, then raise your chin high as you march over to the gate and start using your feet to dominantly rake the ground like a rooster (you don't need to take your shoes off). Dogs do this to spread their scent around. Then walk in and out through the gate in the most leisurely, aloof manner with your chin held high. Yawn and blink slowly.

With this simple bit of play-acting, you're telling Argus, This is MY gate now.

Next, you're going to teach Argus to walk through the gate in a respectful way behind you. Never again are you going to accept him barging and dragging you through. When it's time for the walk, really get into the role of the aloof leader. The cameras are rolling, so let's see if you can be a better actor than your dog. Approach the gate in the most aloof way you can, with your chin held high, occasionally looking down at Argus in warning from the corner of your eye as you say, 'Back!' in a low, commanding voice.

As the temptation of the gate gets closer, walk slower, and insist Argus still stays back behind you. Keep your chin high but continue to watch him from the corner of your eye. Give a leader's growl any time Argus tries to nose in front. All this tells him, I'm not bluffing — I really mean what I say. This is my gate, so I go through first.

At the gate, make Argus sit a few times before getting him to pass through behind you. If Argus insists on still barging through the gate at the last minute, barge him right back. Give him a taste of his own medicine!

With a bit of practice, you'll have a dog that always walks calmly through the gate behind you. That's when you know Argus is treating you with the respect you deserve!

Does your dog wee around your letterbox?

Every time I take my dog Willie for a walk, he stops, sniffs and wees on our letterbox on the way out — and again on the way home. It's disgusting! Why does he do this?

One of the most important jobs of a leader in the Dog World is making sure no intruders try to take over the territory — even when he's not home.

When Willie scent-marks on your letterbox, he's telling the world, Smell this? This is MY gate and MY territory. So — pssssss — all you wannabe challengers out there: STAY OFF MY TERRITORY!

Dogs instinctively refresh this smelly warning as often as they can. If they can escape from your yard, they'll refresh it every morning and evening at the very least. This is because every time another dog scent-marks over Willie's warning, it has to be refreshed.

Willie's using the walk as a perfect excuse to refresh his smelly warning two more times.

The problem with allowing Willie to wee on your letterbox is that you're allowing him to grab the leader's job from you. If you let him scent-mark as you start out on a walk, he'll also assume you're letting him be the Boss of the Walk.

My advice to you is to take over this territorial warning job yourself. Don't worry, I'm not suggesting you use Willie's methods! Rather, act like a rooster and scratch your feet around the ground near your letterbox. Your feet will do a good job of scent-marking, even if you're wearing shoes. Your scent-mark is now the territorial warning to other dogs, and it lets everyone, including Willie, know who the new boss of this territory is — you.

If Willie disputes your claim to guard the territory by disrespectfully weeing on the letterbox as usual, immediately march through him as though he's not there, repeat your scratching performance and briskly walk on.

If you can't be bothered pretending to scent-mark your territory, just make sure Willie doesn't either. Drag him past your letterbox at a fast pace and don't let him stop.

Now Willie can't grab control of the walk by weeing on the letterbox.

Does your dog endlessly stop and sniff?

My dog Snuff wastes half our walk by stopping to leisurely sniff at different spots. It drives me nuts. I want to walk, but she wants to sniff — we'll never get a decent walk this way. Am I being unreasonable?

By stopping the walk whenever she wants to sniff something, Snuff is trying to make herself the Boss of the Walk. It's actually a very leisurely way of dominating you.

It's not that there's nothing to sniff — there are always plenty of interesting smells out there — but Snuff's taken it upon herself to be the one who decides when and what you stop to smell. However, these decisions should be the privilege of the leader — and that should be you. If you go on letting her stop and sniff, you're telling her, That's okay, Snuff — I don't mind if you want to be the boss.

Snuff is also telling any other dog that may be watching:

See who's in charge around here? It's me. We don't move along until I say we do. Hold on, human ... I just want to answer this pee-mail ... and this one ... and, yeah, this interesting one over here.

So what's a reasonable compromise for letting your dog sniff out on the walk? I believe dogs need to sniff their environment. The walk is their main information-gathering time of the day. However, it should be your decision as the leader as to what you should stop to sniff. I don't mind if dogs sniff as they walk along — they just can't keep stopping the walk.

By the way, if you want to really show why you should be Boss of the Walk because of your superior smelling powers, pretend to stop and sniff something amazing on the ground. Sniff at a certain spot in a fascinated manner. Pretend to taste the smell at the front of your mouth and sneeze, then sniff the spot again.

Now Snuff will look at you with respect, thinking, Gee, I can't smell anything special — you must have an amazingly superior sense of smell! End your little pantomime by scratching at the spot with your feet, keeping your chin raised.

What you've just said is, Give up your pathetic attempts to dominate me by sniffing, Snuff, because my superior nose wins hands down. I'm the leader around here.

Don't let Snuff sniff her way into being Boss of the Walk!

Who's the boss of the leash?

My dog Buster is a total nightmare to walk because he won't stop dragging me around. How can I stop him when he's so strong?

Why is Buster so intent on dragging you around on that leash? A lot of dogs will quite calmly walk on the leash without pulling, but some dogs were born to try to be the boss — and your dog is obviously one of them.

What Buster is telling you as he drags you around is, Ha! I'm going to prove my dominance over you by winning this moving tug-of-war game. If I can really pull you along — then I'm clearly proving I'm the Boss of the Walk.

This is one of those really important challenges you must win. Dogs that pull on the leash are a nightmare to walk.

First, get Buster in a more submissive frame of mind before you even start the walk. Call him to you and get him to sit. Raise your chin as you bend down to clip his leash on.

Now you're going to teach him to walk behind you until he respects you. This way he can't drag you along.

I suggest you practice walking Buster around your backyard first. Walk around the yard in a firm, calm manner with your chin raised to show how in control you are. Pretend Buster's invisible. If you keep intently watching him, patting him or talking to him, he'll feel far too important. It will seem as though you're asking him to be your boss, so act aloofly instead.

As you walk, every now and then remind him to stay back. Your dog is going to learn that 'Back!' now means: Stay back politely behind me. Don't walk in front of me.

The moment Buster tries to overtake you, barge sideways into him so he goes back behind you. He may dart backwards and pretend to be extremely shocked, but this is all an act. He's just hoping to have you stop and submissively fuss over him. Instead of falling for his theatrical tricks, pretend nothing unusual is happening and keep walking with him behind you.

Without looking at him, raise your chin and keep firmly reminding him to stay back behind you. From the corner of your eye, watch for him to edge up and overtake you. As soon as he tries to pass, barge him so he drops back behind you again.

However, if Buster keeps trying to overtake you in a very pushy, dominant way, raise your chin higher and turn and march straight into him so he's stepping and jumping backwards. After forcing him to get quick smart out of your way for a few metres, I want you to turn around and walk off again. This time Buster should submissively fall in behind you.

Once Buster's walking calmly and respectfully behind you, then you're ready to take him out in public. Make sure he walks through your front gate behind you. Don't let him scent-mark around your gateway. Raise your chin and keep reminding him to stay back behind you.

Now you're off your property, practice having Buster walk respectfully behind you no matter what distractions are happening around him. The more dominant he is the more he'll try to overtake you, but don't let him.

If Buster tries to overtake, barge into him so he falls straight back behind you. If he's being particularly dominant, march straight into him so he's walking and jumping submissively back out of your way. When he seems to have stopped trying to challenge you, turn and walk away so he falls in politely behind you.

After about three weeks, Buster will stop challenging you as much and will accept he has to walk submissively behind you no matter what distractions are going on around him. You should now have a dog that's very easy to walk!

Moving on up

I followed your suggestions about walking Buster in the 'Back' position and they worked. I can now walk him easily out in public without him trying to overtake me all the time. How can I now teach Buster to walk in front of me without pulling on the leash?

Congratulations on your hard work so far! Now it's time to allow Buster some freedom by teaching him to walk out in front of you without pulling on the leash. However, be warned: your dog is really going to test who's controlling the walk once he's allowed out in front of you.

After walking with him in the submissive 'Back' position for about five minutes, let Buster walk out in front of you by giving a new command: 'Walk on'. This means: You can walk on a loose leash in front of me — but only as long as you don't pull on the leash at all.

He'll be a little confused at first but keep repeating this new command in a happy voice until he overtakes you. When he walks in front of you, say warmly, 'Walk on. Good boy.'

However, the instant Buster pulls even a tiny bit on the leash, jerk it and sternly say, 'Don't pull!'

Repeat until Buster learns he can't get away with pulling on the leash at all. You should jerk him at the slightest pressure. He'll probably test you nonstop the first day — and plenty more times for three weeks — but stay calm and inexhaustible.

Keep an eye out for any of Buster's dominating little tricks as he tussles with you for the right to control the walk from the front. For example, don't let him try to control the walk by veering off the footpath to wee, scent-mark or sniff. Don't let him set the pace of the walk, either. After a week of practice, you should be able to hold the leash loosely and slow your pace right down without Buster pulling on the leash. So keep your chin up and become vigilant about warning him not to pull on the leash at all. The second he tries to test you, jerk his leash and sternly warn him, 'Don't pull!'

If he's really ignoring you and you're getting frustrated, teach him to respect you more by raising your chin and marching straight into him so he's walking and jumping backwards submissively out of your way. Now turn and walk off again, firmly saying, 'Walk on.'

After a few more tests, he'll work out that you're not going to accept any more rude, dominant behaviour. Even though you're letting Buster walk out in front he needs to respect that you're now the Boss of the Walk.

After you've followed these instructions vigilantly for about three weeks, Buster should be a beautiful dog to walk on the leash. You'll be able to hold the leash loosely and walk at any pace you want, and he still won't pull you at all.

Is your dog using the leash to pull you off balance?

My dog Cedric is very big and bouncy and strong. You're going to think I'm paranoid but I think he springs around deliberately to try to pull me off balance. He keeps jerking my sore back at odd angles and it really hurts! What do you think I can do to stop this?

You're not being paranoid. Big, bouncy dogs like Cedric love springing around in an effort to get the right angle to jerk the leash. He's deliberately trying to pull you off balance. Unbalancing someone is a very dominant thing to do in the Dog World, as well as dangerous for you, so you can't let Cedric keep doing this.

Why is he doing it? As Cedric knows you're competing with him to be the Boss of the Walk, he observes you closely to work out your weaknesses so he can work out how to beat you. Dogs are natural-born predators so they're extremely talented at discerning weaknesses. They can always spot any injuries their owners may have because the owner will be walking differently.

Cedric's obviously deduced your weak spot is your sore back. Now he's using the leash to test how much control he can grab off you. All he has to do is bounce around you to find out which angles easily pull you off balance and jerk your back. The more he hurts your back, the more control you helplessly hand over to him.

However, Cedric's not being a bad dog. He's just a naturally exuberant, strong dog who can't help testing your strengths and weaknesses out on the walk. Remember, as soon as a dog spots a weakness in you he'll test you to find out exactly how weak you are. This is a survival instinct in your dog.

To prevent Cedric hurting your back any further, you must stop him bouncing around. Make Cedric walk behind you sedately in the 'Back' position (explained on page 192). There are special leash products available that will help you keep him calmly walking behind you.

It will help Cedric walk sedately behind you if you keep your chin raised as you slowly yawn and sleepily blink. Keep repeating the command 'Back'. The calmer you are, the calmer he'll become.

You can also help get him into a naturally more submissive mood by constantly commanding him to sit. Getting energetic dogs to sit for you repeatedly soon bores them into better behaviour.

I also think Cedric needs more exercise to calm him down. I find if you take big, strong energetic dogs swimming off-leash every day, they get really exhausted. Perhaps you could try this.

From now on, don't let Cedric dominantly weave and bounce around on the end of his leash. Use the special harness and your gentle, relaxed manner to persuade Cedric that this is just a relaxed walk in the park — you're not his personal jumping castle!

My dog won't come back when she's off the leash

When I'm down at the park I often find my dog Daisy won't come back when I call her. I stand there calling her for ages, feeling like a fool, but if I try to walk towards her, she simply runs off. What can I do?

For Daisy, this has become a great game of Follow the Leader. The only problem is she believes she's the leader!

Daisy has to learn that you're now clever enough to get her to come back on command. For a start, practice getting Daisy to come back to you while she's on a very long leash.

Use a scratch behind the ear as her reward for returning on your command.

If Daisy doesn't want to return to you on the long leash, put her in a more submissive mood first by using the three commands 'Come', 'Sit' and 'Stay' repeatedly and rewarding her with food treats when she obeys you.

Once she's coming back for you on the long leash, try practising off-leash in your backyard. If she returns easily to you there, try getting her to return to you in a more open space, such as the local park.

If freedom in such a big area gets her overexcited and she won't come back to you, try crouching down and let your hands rest on the ground while you sway playfully from side to side. Now call Daisy to you in a playful voice. In the Dog World, this is a fun invitation to come over and play.

When she reaches you, raise your chin, clip her back on her leash and stand up to avoid being jumped on.

When 'crouch and play' doesn't work for Daisy

I followed all the suggestions in the last answer, but when I tried to get Daisy to return to me by acting playful, she just stood and watched me from a distance. What else can I try?

If the 'crouch and play' tactic isn't Daisy's cup of tea, try sniffing the air and excitedly running off to a spot nearby, pretending that you've discovered something really wonderful and delicious to smell or eat. You might make-believe it's a mouse you're catching. See if you can turn in an Oscar-winning performance as you pantomime catching that tiny rodent. Believe me, you really can't overact in the Dog World!

As you sniff at that fascinating mystery animal you've just caught in your cupped hands, really sound excited about it. Don't keep looking at Daisy, as this will only make her suspect a trick. If your acting is good enough, she'll be curious enough to investigate what's got you so fascinated.

When Daisy comes over, praise her lavishly and pretend to eat a tidbit and drop it at her feet. While she's eating, you can calmly hold her collar and clip her back on her leash if you need to.

For those really stubborn dogs that just won't come back to you (usually very energetic breeds that aren't getting enough exercise), why let them off the leash in the first place?

If Daisy constantly ruins your walk by refusing to return, then make your life easier: keep her on a long leash at all times and just make your walk longer.

Too many pats down the street

Why does my dog Prince become so disobedient when I walk him on a leash around our busy local shops? He's quite well behaved at home and down at the park, but once I walk down that busy street and start talking to people, he really starts pulling on the leash and ignoring me. He's such a friendly, handsome dog that everyone likes to pat and admire him, but it's so embarrassing when he starts ignoring me so publicly. Why does he do this to me?

The problem is not you; it's all the people who stop to pat and admire Prince. Every pat he scores off some unsuspecting human at your local shops makes him think he's much more important than you — so therefore he doesn't have to bother obeying you any more.

As another person pats him down the street, he thinks, Aha! Another pat means I earn another point ... gee, I feel important today. That's fourteen humans I've scored pats from today. I even tricked most of them into patting me submissively on the chest and under the chin just by gently raising my chin high. Ha! Since I've now won so many points I can now ignore my own human because I've clearly proved I'm the boss. After all, none of those strangers are bending down and patting my human submissively, are they?

To stop Prince collecting all these unhealthy pats from humans, ask him to sit submissively at your heel whenever you stop and talk to people. If anyone's interested in Prince, politely explain that any human attention feeds his megalomania complex. Say the best thing they can do is to completely ignore him and pretend he doesn't exist.

Sorry, Prince, but your ego is ballooning out of control with all this extra attention — so no more pats in public for you.

Control concerns

Call me paranoid, but I don't think I have enough control of my dog Sean if I take him off the leash. Am I cruel not letting him go free down at the park?

I think you should listen to any cautious instincts you have; I find my own pretty reliable. If you don't feel confident about Sean's behaviour off-leash then it's probably for a good reason. If you're scared of him causing problems down at the park with other dogs and people, then it's perfectly okay to keep him on his leash whenever you take him out in public. Simply walk him for longer on an extra-long leash.

I've found that humans are obsessed with giving their dogs too much freedom! Freedom for some dogs often ends up in drama.

When I go out to help solve a behaviour problem that's happened off-leash, I always hear the owner say, 'My dog's never done this before.'

Unfortunately, a dog only has to make one aggressive mistake to land himself in a lot of trouble. So listen to your instincts and prevent trouble from happening.

Build a big fenced yard for Sean to have freedom at home and get in the habit of walking him twice a day — in the morning and evening. Don't let Sean go free when you're in public. Difficult dogs are definitely safer and more enjoyable to walk when they stay clipped on their leash.

One of my favourite mottos is 'Better safe than sorry'.

Are you still having trouble winning the battle of the walk?

I've been following your advice about the most common challenges on the walk, and how to stop my dog Josh from totally dominating me, but it's been seven days now and I think he's actually getting worse! What am I doing wrong?

If Josh is an extremely dominant personality, don't expect him to hand you control of the walk after only seven days.

He worked incredibly hard to become Boss of the Walk, so he's not going to give it up without a struggle!

Think of how many times he's won these walking challenges against you. Maybe twice a day over months — or even years? I find it takes at least a month or so for a very pushy dog to see how serious you are about making yourself the Boss of the Walk.

Sometimes a dog like Josh actually starts challenging you even more when he sees you're trying to take his leadership away from him. This is his last desperate attempt to hang on to his control over you. But take heart: if he's challenging you more, it shows you've got him rattled and you're winning. Otherwise he'd just be contemptuously treating you the same as normal.

All you can do is stay calm, firm and inexhaustibly determined to win. If you look flustered, exhausted, angry or stressed, then Josh will fight even harder to win control of the walk. Until you look confident and calm he won't trust you to be in charge out in public. Be inexhaustible rather than angry — this attitude always impresses dogs!

Don't worry, Josh has to play by the rules of the Dog World. If you win all the walking challenges for long enough then you'll eventually earn the right to be the Boss of the Walk. At the moment he's just testing you as far as he can in the hope you'll give up and let him be the boss again.

I understand some dogs are exhausting to win challenges against but please don't give up after all your hard work. What's three weeks — or even three months — of training compared to the many years you're going to own this dog?

The rules of the Dog World are simple: if you keep

notching up enough wins with all the walking challenges Josh has to concede defeat and hand over control of the walk to you. With a very pushy dog, don't expect to see much improvement before a month of hard testing has passed. Some extremely dominant dogs may continue to test you for as long as three months.

If you have a dog this dominant, you must try to win as many of the challenges in this book as possible. Extremely dominant dogs mustn't win any challenges — it just makes them too stubborn.

Hopefully, the time Josh is prepared to test you to your limits will pass very quickly. Good luck!

8

Difficult Dogs

Every now and again you come across a really difficult dog that resists giving up its problem behaviours. If your dog is particularly difficult, then this section may help you decide your best and safest course of action.

Dog-sitting dilemma

My friend Jack has kindly offered to stay at my house and look after my dog Bella for two weeks while I go away on holidays. But will he accidentally undo all the training I've put into her lately? Jack's a bit of a softie and Bella can be very bossy and naughty when she wants to be. What do you think I should do?

I would listen to your doubts: I believe it would be a mistake to leave Bella at home with Jack while you're away.

If Jack's a softie with dogs, then he's probably going to let Bella do whatever she wants. As soon as she spots Jack's a pushover, Bella will get to work to topple him as the leader because he's obviously too weak to be left in charge. She'll try to dethrone him by throwing nonstop challenges at him until she earns enough victories to be his undisputed boss.

Think about it: you know all Bella's worst challenges — do you really want her trying them all on soft-hearted Jack? Pushy, dominant dogs can be very unpleasant to dog-sit. You risk leaving your friend in charge of a naughty, out-of-control dog while you're away. It also means you'll have to teach Bella good, respectful manners all over again on your return.

Worse, if Bella's used aggression in the past, she may also try to start a fight with another dog out in public. She'll do this as a way of grabbing the leadership from helpless Jack. Bella might even show aggression to Jack once she's won enough challenges from him. For all these reasons, I believe a reputable dog boarding kennel is the safest place for Bella.

The good news is that sending a dominant dog like Bella away for a few weeks will actually be good for her. Being sent away from the pack is one way you can make a dog more subservient and respectful, because when it returns, the dog naturally believes it's the least important member of the pack. All you have to do is keep treating Bella as the least important member of your household and she'll continue behaving beautifully.

Laundry-day blues

I decided to wash my dog Missy's bed blankets today — and something horrific happened. I gently tried to shoo her off her blankets, but she didn't budge. When I tried to pull the blankets from under her, she growled and snapped at me. Her teeth only grazed my arm but it shocked me terribly. What did I do wrong? I was only trying to wash her blankets!

When you tried to pull her blankets from under her, Missy thought, Stop touching my important leader's bed! How dare you try to steal my bedding! Dogs don't understand about washing blankets — Missy just saw another pack member trying to steal her precious bedding.

It's a huge shock when the dog you've done so much for tries to bluff-attack you like this. However, dogs do have to earn the right to be aggressive towards you. If Missy gave you a warning snap then she clearly thinks she's your boss. This is a dangerous attitude we have to change as soon as possible.

It's time to stop spoiling Missy with so much attention and affection. She sees your constant kindness as weakness, so now it's time for you to make yourself the boss of Missy. From now on, I want you to be very aloof with your dog until she starts treating you with more respect.

For example: ignore her much more; don't do things for her all the time; don't watch her constantly; keep your chin raised around her; and stop patting and touching her nonstop. All these suggestions will help stop Missy from feeling so important, but I'd also like you to read through this book several times to see what other challenges you might be losing to her.

You'll probably have to be very aloof around her for at least three weeks before she believes that you're no longer her submissive follower. However, some very dominant dogs will need to be ignored for even longer.

I still want you to walk Missy and spend time around her. Just stop treating her as though she's the most important thing in the world.

Next time you have to wash Missy's blankets, I suggest you secure her on a leash in another room while you feed her a treat. While she's safely tethered you can go back to her sleeping area and deal with the blankets at your leisure. Do the same when the blankets are dried and you have to replace them on her bed.

As for the blankets she's already guarded so aggressively from you, throw them out or they'll make her feel far too important. It's much better to buy new ones that you're the boss of.

Now laundry days won't be scary days.

Today's hormone surges

Some days my teenage dog, Jake, is naughtier than others. Why?

Just like human teenagers, dog teenagers can get really strong hormone surges some days. This gives them such powerful bursts of energy that they can't help challenging you more than usual. On such days, simply reduce the amount of freedom and attention you give Jake. That way Jake will have fewer opportunities to win challenges against you.

It will help if you act in a very aloof manner on his bad hormone-surge days. This is how lead dogs would behave around a particularly pushy teenager, so raise your chin high — and more often!

I suggest you also give Jake raw bones to chew on surge days to tire him out. Increase his exercise on those days, too, so he stays too exhausted to misbehave. Swimming, by the way, really tires out naughty teenage dogs.

So don't take a surge in Jake's naughtiness personally. Teenagers of all species have no control over their hormones!

Why can't I let my dog swing from a hanging tyre?

I've heard you say on the radio you don't believe in letting dogs swing from hanging tyres. Why? My dog Toby absolutely loves this game!

I know some dog breeds love playing this game, in which dogs grip a hanging tyre or plastic ring with their strong jaws, but I've also seen what happens when these dogs mature. It can all too easily turn deadly.

The hunting instinct this game brings out in Toby is a very dangerous one — it's the dramatic pull the big game animal to the ground so we can kill it instinct. No dog should ever be encouraged to use this instinct, even in play. It's simply too dangerous.

Why? When dogs play games, they practice and improve their hunting and fighting skills. The skills they practice the most stay close to the surface, ready to be used when needed. Think about it: do you really want Toby having this deadly killing skill ready to use at a moment's notice? By the time Toby matures, you don't want him trained to use his teeth to drag prey to the ground in a killing hold. I think you'll agree this is not a safe skill to encourage in any dog.

If something happens one day to suddenly trigger Toby's adrenaline and he gets overexcited, frightened or angry, you have no idea which weapon he'll instinctively pull out of his arsenal. Dogs can't think sensibly when they're fuelled on adrenaline — they just react instantly. Don't give Toby the chance to treat a child or another dog like that hanging tyre. The result would be catastrophic.

Allowing dogs to play with hanging tyres is extremely dangerous, so please prevent Toby from playing this game forever.

The scary day your dog fully matures

I'm still in shock. My dog Trigger did something down at the park today that he's never done before. One moment he was playing happily, the next he'd erupted into an enormous fight with another dog. My hands are still shaking at the memory. Why on earth did he do it? He's just turned four and is desexed.

It's often a shock for owners when their dog becomes fully mature. This is because it can happen without warning. Unfortunately, some owners only realise their dog is acting differently when — like Trigger — their dog has its first intense dog fight.

What caused the fight? Trigger may have won the right to be the boss over the other dog down at the park. But if the other dog refused to accept this, Trigger may have decided to teach it a lesson by attacking it. Full maturity gives some dogs the confidence and drive to settle things with a serious fight if they have to.

So be prepared: your newly mature dog may use aggression again in the future. The more dominant his personality, the more often this will happen.

There are signs that your dog is about to reach maturity. Learn to watch out for a new super-confidence in your dog. Watch out for other warning signs, too, such as more scent-marking, more aggression, more frequent examples of pushy behaviour, more acting aloofly around you, and less tolerance of other dogs challenging him.

I suggest you keep Trigger on a leash when he's out in public. If he's used aggression before then he'll probably use aggression again. Better safe than sorry. From now on, too, always supervise Trigger around children and visitors. Definitely stop him from playing any games that encourage pushy, aggressive behaviour, such as wrestling, tug of war, chasing, or jumping up to hang off a suspended tyre.

Make sure, too, that you start using plenty of calming signals around Trigger that let him know you're the leader and you're always fully in control. Raise your chin higher than before and relax him by yawning slowly and blinking sleepily while turning your head away.

When you have a fully mature dog like Trigger that's not afraid to use aggression you must become extremely serious about always being in control. Never allow your dog to discipline other dogs and humans. He's not the leader, so this isn't his job.

Be aware that this is not a problem that will simply fade away with time. From now on, it's your job as leader to always keep Trigger under complete control out in public, or he'll become a ticking time bomb waiting to explode into another fight.

Is your dog using aggression to grab control of the walk?

Help! My dog Bubba is starting to get very aggressive out on the walk, rushing off and barking at other dogs. What should I do?

Bubba can sense you don't feel completely in control while out on a walk. And as he rushes off barking aggressively at another dog, he gets the perfect opportunity to prove you can't control him.

As he races away from you, barking aggressively, he's telling everyone, Ha! I know how to grab the leadership from my human — WOOF! WOOF! WOOF! Get back from me, everyone! I'm the most powerful boss around here and I can behave exactly how I like! Who's going to stop me intimidating everyone? Come on — are there any challengers around here?

From now on, bully-boy Bubba definitely stays on a leash out in public. Taking away his freedom by putting him on a leash is the most powerful way you can remain his boss.

Bubba can have freedom when he's in your secure backyard or in his dog pen.

How do we stop Bubba barking aggressively at other dogs while he's on the leash? Until you have him under much better control, make him stay submissively behind you in the 'Back' position: barge through him the second he tries to overtake you, repeating the command 'Back!'

This stops him thinking he's out 'on point' in front of you — in the natural guarding position. However, you can only barge through Bubba if he doesn't show aggression towards you. For example, don't use this technique if he growls in warning. If Bubba shows you any sort of aggression towards you for barging, then you need to read through this book and solve that issue first.

Now we have to stop Bubba from barking at other dogs. Be aware that every time Bubba makes aggressive noises at another dog he's openly challenging your authority. For this reason I want you to develop zero tolerance to Bubba doing it again.

The moment he whines, growls or barks from behind you at another dog, raise your chin and turn your head just enough so you can glare back at him from the corner of your eye. Jerk his leash sharply and say curtly, 'Leave it!'

Don't shout or scream this command or he'll think you're panicking. If he ignores you and keeps making aggressive noises at the other dog, raise your chin even higher, turn around and walk into him. If he doesn't step back, barge through him so he gets out of your way submissively. Every time you make him step back submissively out of your way, you earn the right to be obeyed a little bit more. Always remember to keep your chin raised as you barge through him.

If you do barge through Bubba, yet he insolently continues to defy your authority by growling and barking at another dog, make the decision that he can't even look at another dog.

Every time he tries, barge straight through him — and

make him go back five or six paces. As soon as you stop, remind him to 'Leave it!'

Eventually Bubba will stop looking at other dogs and will walk submissively beside you. Once he's calmly and quietly ignoring all other dogs no matter what they do, you know you're finally the boss of him out in public. Well done.

Look out, Bubba — your bully days are over!

When your misbehaving dog is on his last chance ... send him away to a boarding kennel

I give up! Our dog Axel is so pushy and stubborn I can't deal with him any more. I know he's been allowed to be the leader for a long time, but despite following your advice I still can't get him to do what I want. I'm ready to take him to the pound. Have you any last suggestions before he goes?

If Axel's stubbornly refusing to hand over the leadership to you there's still one way you can take the leadership off him, and that is by banishing your dog to the furthest wastelands of Outer Siberia: leave him at a boarding kennel for a week. This action gives Axel a clear message: You're being kicked out of the pack for not being respectful. We won't accept your pushy, rude behaviour around here any longer.

When dogs are sent away for a period of time they return to find themselves automatically the least important member of the pack. Once Axel is home, it will be your job to make sure he stays at the bottom of your pack for the rest of his life. How? Don't allow him to win enough challenges to claw his way back up to the top leadership spot.

I want you to make sure Axel's banishment is a very powerful experience. Ensure your family acts in a very cold, aloof way as he's leaving — don't let anyone tearfully fuss over him. Drop him off on your own.

Ask the staff at the boarding kennel to ignore Axel as much as possible so he doesn't win many challenges against them. This means they shouldn't touch him, look at him or speak to him more than can be helped. He can't be given any affection during his stay at the boarding kennel at all. Being coolly ignored is going to help to make him feel much less self-important.

Also, ask the staff to ignore any sad, depressed behaviour, as this shows Axel's rehabilitation is working. What most humans take to be 'sad, depressed' behaviour is actually extremely submissive, polite behaviour in the Dog World. This is what we want to see. It shows Axel is trying to exaggerate how submissive he's being as a way of getting accepted again.

You need to continue being aloof with Axel for a week after you pick him up from the boarding kennel. I call this week 'Ignoring Week'. Being aloof is your way of telling him, You're on probation for showing me disrespect in the past. I don't know if you can stay in our pack yet. I'll see if you behave politely enough.

Your whole family should help you ignore the dog and pretend he's invisible. If everyone excitedly crowds around Axel to welcome him back with pats and happy voices, you are all telling him, Yippee — the boss is back! As you can imagine, this would make Axel go back to his old misbehaving ways very quickly. So keep being very aloof to Axel for the entire seven days of Ignoring Week.

When you bring Axel inside during Ignoring Week, make sure he has no freedom. The best way to do this is to keep him on a secured leash in a corner of the room. This will help him learn new, polite manners while he's indoors. Being on a leash will also stop him from walking around challenging everyone. If he won't settle on his leash, put him back outside or take him for a walk to tire him out.

After Ignoring Week is over I want you to judge how Axel's behaving. Is he showing signs of being polite, respectful and submissive? If he is, then your hard work has paid off. You can unclip Axel when you trust him to behave. As soon as he misbehaves, clip him back on his leash in the corner or put him outside.

You can show Axel more affection gradually but only as long as he's being polite to you. As soon as he starts being unruly and pushy go back to being aloof until he learns he's definitely not more important than you.

If Axel's still too pushy for you to cope with after he's been banished to a boarding kennel for a week — as well as been ignored for another week on his return — then I don't think Axel is the right dog for you. He's obviously a very dominant personality and needs a firm owner with the willpower to deal with his constant challenges.

If this is the case, I suggest you contact your vet and discuss your options for re-homing Axel. Perhaps they can put you in contact with a reputable dog-rescue shelter.

Hopefully, however, my solution will work well for Axel. It's designed to give you a much more submissive dog that's easier to win challenges against. You still need to stay his boss every day for the rest of his life — but this method just gives you a bit of a helping hand to get started.

Can dogs be cured of aggression towards humans?

Our dog Sasha has grown quite aggressive over the years and we're concerned because she nipped a visitor the other day. She's four years old, desexed and a well-known guarding breed. After hearing you on the radio, we realise we're probably responsible for this problem because we did all the wrong things with her — making her feel too important and letting her playfully nip us. Lately, however, we've seen her aggression become much more serious towards people outside the family. Do you think her aggression can be cured or is it too late?

In my experience, once Sasha has learned to use aggression to get her own way, then she'll resort to using aggression again sooner or later. I believe she really can't be trusted not to bite anyone again.

Even if you bring in major behavioural changes, Sasha may behave well for months or even years but then — bang! — you could find yourself involved in a horrific aggression incident with her.

You're already concerned about her unreliable behaviour around non-family members. I believe you should listen to your instincts. For this reason, I suggest you now seriously consider whether Sasha is going to be too great a risk to continue owning. In my opinion she is.

Are you really prepared to risk a more serious bite

situation or, even worse, an attack on another dog, child or adult? Are you willing to risk the emotional, legal and financial nightmare if the worst should happen?

I know the idea of putting Sasha to sleep is extremely distressing. However, a dog attack can happen in just a few minutes and the results can be horrific. We've all read terrifying headlines: CHILD MAULED TO DEATH BY DOG; NEIGHBOUR KILLED BY DOG; WALKER BADLY SAVAGED BY DOG. These dogs all had owners like you who probably never thought these tragedies would ever happen to them — but unfortunately they did. You don't want the next tragic newspaper headline to be about Sasha.

I believe the safest course of action with a dog that is openly aggressive to people is to have it euthanised — re-homing is not an option in these cases. Many people will disagree with me on this, but I believe the safety of humans comes first, every time.

As I've learned, you may be the best-intentioned owner in the world, but everyone makes mistakes occasionally. Accidents happen. Dogs get through fences. Kids get into dog enclosures. Neighbours spark arguments. Visitors do the wrong thing. The other dog is the one that started the fight.

If Sasha has no fear of biting humans, then I'm afraid she's already reached the point of no return. Please listen to your instincts and common sense. You never want to have the tragedy of a dog attack on a human on your conscience. I strongly suggest you discuss Sasha's options with a vet you trust as soon as possible.

Just another tragic love story

My little dog Babe was a cute, fluffy dog we bought as a puppy from the pet shop. Sadly, she turned out to be a bad choice. Although we gave her lots of affection and love from the day she came home, she turned very nasty and became aggressive to us. Unfortunately, we had to get her put down when she was two years old because she ended up nipping too many people. Now I want to buy another little toy breed because they're so cute and fun — but how can I avoid picking another aggressive personality?

Every year, many small fluffy dogs are euthanised for showing aggression. This is sad because little dogs like Babe become aggressive if everyone makes them feel too important.

That's right, Babe was a victim of her own cuteness. All that love and affection you gave her every day did one thing — It made her the undisputed boss of your household. As a result, she started nipping people when they didn't act submissively enough around her.

I'm concerned that if you buy another cute little fluffy puppy, you're going to make all the same mistakes again. Please don't spoil your next little dog by giving it too much attention and treating it as if it's the most important member of your family.

Another reason small, cute dogs easily become our boss is because we let them get away with doing pretty much what they want. We allow them to go anywhere they want in our house, so they race around inside, feeling as if they own this very important inner-den area. We let them dominantly sleep on our bed, lie on the couch and sit on our laps. We submissively carry them around. We submissively give them too many pats and treats. We constantly take Submissive Steps over to them. We watch them far too much. We let them dominantly jump up on our legs. We also let them get away with barking dominantly all around our territory. You get the idea: it's so dangerously easy to spoil little dogs.

But little fluffy dogs should live by exactly the same rules as big dogs. Always treat any dog — no matter how small, cute and fluffy — as the least important member of your family.

I hope you now realise Babe wasn't a bad dog. She was just acting like a leader and making sure she was treated with the respect she deserved. Now it's up to you to ensure this tragic story doesn't happen again. Please don't be tempted to overindulge your next little cute dog and let it win challenge after challenge until it becomes your boss. Tragically, vets euthanise little fluffy boss dogs every day for aggressively insisting they be respected as the boss. Cuteness can kill little dogs.

9

Some Last Questions ...

What happens if you try some of the ideas in this book and you don't get much success? If you have a particularly stubborn, pushy dog that constantly ignores you, then believe me, this section is especially relevant for you. In this final section I've listed twenty-five ways your dog is still earning the right to ignore your commands. The good news is that once you win back these challenges, your dog will automatically start to obey you. These powerful challenges are the way all wise dog leaders win ultimate control of the pack, even if they have to deal with the most rebellious dogs.

Why does my dog keep challenging me nonstop?

Why does my dog Elvis keep throwing challenges at me when I just want to be his friend?

Dogs and humans don't see friendship in the same way. Even if Elvis really likes you, he'll always throw challenges at you.

He can't help doing this — it's how dogs were designed by Mother Nature to survive. Naturally dominant dogs like Elvis simply throw out more challenges than other dogs.

This means Elvis will try to tread on your toes more often. He'll try to lean against you more often. Barge into you more than other dogs would. You get the idea. He's just a naturally pushy personality.

Why does Elvis bother throwing so many challenges at you? In the Dog World, if you win a challenge, then you score a point. The dog who scores the most points, earns the right to be the leader. It's a way dogs decide who's the most capable boss without having to fight each other all the time. This simple point system works brilliantly for dogs.

I now want you to start winning challenges against Elvis so you start building up your own point score. If you want him to behave for you, you've got to earn more points than he does. This will make you his leader. You can still be Elvis's friend, but you must always be his leader.

Below, I've listed twenty-five of the most popular challenges dogs use to dominate humans. These are what I call the classic challenges of the Dog World. The Dog World is a very simple place: if Elvis wins enough of these challenges against you, then he wins enough points to be your boss.

The twenty-five most popular challenges your dog will throw at you

Ask yourself: are you winning these classic challenges, or is your dog? (Every victory equals one point.)

1. Who's grabbing everyone's attention any way they can?

This is one of the simplest ways to notch up lots of points. You can bark and get everyone looking at you. You can show off. You can race around and get others watching you out of curiosity. You can look cute so others just stare at you in admiration.

2. Who's making the most noise?

Barking loudly, scratching noisily at doors, and deliberately pounding around heavily on wooden floors are all ways you can dominate using noise.

3. Who gets others to pat them whenever they demand it?

It is an especially powerful victory if you can get others to touch you in submissive places, such as under the chin, on the throat and on the chest.

4. Who gets the best sleeping and resting spots?

You get extra points if you can grab the big bed in the main bedroom, or the best couch in the house.

5. Who controls all the narrow thoroughfares around your home — such as the doorways, hallways, stairways, verandahs and gateways?

You can easily notch up points in these areas by being first through them, or blocking them, or lying across them, or tripping others over as they pass through.

6. Who controls the walk?

You can score lots of points on the walk by dragging others around on the end of the leash. By choosing how fast or slow you'll force others to walk. By choosing when and where to stop and sniff or scent-mark. You can also notch up extra points every time you refuse to come back when you're called to get your leash clipped on.

7. Who controls the visitors?

You can win plenty of victory points by being the first to greet them, jumping up on them, tripping them over, barging into them, demanding pats from them, blocking their right of way and barking at them noisily.

8. Who roams wherever they want inside the house?

This is the important inner-den area where most challenges take place. Having freedom in this area is a very powerful thing as so many points are won and lost here. The most important rooms are the kitchen, the living room and the main bedroom.

9. Who's learned to act very nervously so others let them get away with things?

This is one of the most subtle ways victory points are won.

10. Who uses their smallness, cuteness and apparent helplessness to be carried up high in arms, sit on laps and sleep on beds just like human babies?

The smaller and fluffier you are, the more you seem to get away with.

11. Who controls the food?

You can win lots of points if you take tidbits out of hands, or if you get to eat dry food from a bowl whenever you feel like it. You can also win points by tricking others into spoonfeeding you, stealing food from neighbours or deliberately leaving your food uneaten so you can aggressively guard it.

12. Who wins any tug-of-war and wrestling games by using strength, tenacity and even nips?

Unfortunately, this encourages the most dangerous killing instincts to stay close to the surface, ready to use at a moment's notice.

13. Who ends up with all the toys, balls, old bones and sticks, and leaves them around as victory trophies for everyone to admire?

And look out anyone cheeky enough to try to steal them!

14. Who uses aggression, including growls, nips or even bites, to get their own way?

This is when your dominance is so dangerous you become a risk to humans.

15. Who scent-marks, urinates and poos around the inside of the house to let you know who really owns this territory?

This is incredibly dominant behaviour.

16. Who roams outside the territory whenever they feel like it — often scent-marking all around the neighbourhood?

Having this sort of freedom makes you feel extremely important.

17. Who decides who should be barred from entering the territory by guarding the entrance way?

This instantly makes you the boss of visitors.

18. Who takes over whenever something unusual happens?

You can use lots of barking noise, racing around, jumping up and demanding pats to take over from everyone else.

19. Who's the first to be greeted on waking or when the owner comes home?

Sometimes others can hand you this victory because they act as if they don't care about anyone else in the household.

20. Who grabs control of situations by creating noisy chaos?

Barking is like an invasion of eardrums! It can be too distracting to think clearly when there's lots of noise going on.

21. Who stands still and waits so that others are tempted to take Submissive Steps towards them?

This is subtle manoeuvring indeed!

22. Who acts aloof and ignores everyone as a way of getting extra attention?

Again, a rather subtle, clever ploy to put yourself in charge.

23. Who takes the personal space of others by leaning on them, or stepping on their toes, or licking their face and body in a dominant way?

If you can grab control of someone else's personal space, then you've also earnt the right to be more dominant.

24. Who jumps up and plants their front paws high up on someone else to show their domination?

The higher you can place your own scent-mark on someone else's body, the more dominant you are.

25. Who constantly scent-marks around the boundary and entrance of the pack territory, to make sure their scent is the strongest smelling?

The most dominant scent-mark on the territory tells everone who the most dominant individual is.

A Final Word

Congratulations — you've finished the book!

As you can see, the Dog World's actually a very simple, organised place. I believe if anyone asked, *What's your dog telling you?* your dog's answer would simply be, Just be a good leader for me.

After reading this book, you now know how to be a great leader. So go and enjoy life with your dog!

Acknowledgments

I'd like to thank the fantastic humans in my pack: Lee, Siggy, Casey, Fintan and Marie — I love you all so dearly.

As well, I'd like to thank my own dogs. Life's never boring with you lot around to keep me on my toes.

I'd also like to thank the really impressive lead dogs I've known over the years: you've all taught me basically everything I know — especially you, Jack.

Thanks, too, to my very supportive triplet brothers, John and Andrew and, of course, to Mammy, who was a very special woman.